One of the most tragic pligh
may fall is the absence of assu
grounded assurance of salva
with the trials and temptatic
experiences—our obedience, l
provide us with assurance, but we become stymied by our many
inconsistencies and failings. Thankfully and correctively, *Home
Safe* offers us a rich treasury of wisdom from the past that directs
us to look to the mighty acts of our triune God and the truths of
His Word as the proper basis for assurance of salvation. For all who
struggle in this area, this book will cheer and guide.

Gregg R. Allison

Professor of Christian Theology, The Southern Baptist Theological
Seminary, Louisville, Kentucky

The Spirit of God enables a believer to have an infallible assurance
of faith that is grounded upon God's promises and, even when it is
shaken, have it revived by the Word of God. To renew and attain
such assurance, the Christian should have in his possession a
treasure chest containing the gold of such promises at his ready
disposal. *Home Safe* offers an overflowing trove of teaching and
encouragement on the assurances the Lord has given to His people.

Barry York

President and Professor of Pastoral Theology and Homiletics, Reformed
Presbyterian Theological Seminary, Pittsburgh, Pennsylvania

With a deft touch, Roger Ibrahim has selected the most helpful
words of pastoral theologians of the past on the issue of assurance.
These quotations deserve to be memorized and used again and
again in counsel with those who struggle with assurance of salvation. A most helpful addition.

Derek W. H. Thomas

Senior Minister, First Presbyterian Church, Columbia, South Carolina
Chancellor's Professor, Reformed Theological Seminary
Teaching Fellow, Ligonier Ministries

Assurance of our salvation is the foundation and fountain of joy for Christians. And for that very reason Satan attacks our assurance from many different angles. But this book is like body armour. It covers all the bases by way of protecting us from the devil's bullets. Here we have wise pastoral counsel for troubled souls from great men of the past, astutely set in context by Roger Ibrahim. It will warm any Christian's heart with the love of Jesus and help many pastors to encourage their people.

John Benton
Director for Pastoral Support, Pastors' Academy,
London Seminary

Roger Ibrahim has produced a fascinating little treasure trove of quotes to inject renewed confidence into our often faltering souls. This is not a series of superficial 'one liners'. Each entry, alongside Ibrahim's judicious commentary, could form the basis of a meaty devotional, or preachers could select a few for a sermon series. Doing further research on each of these spiritual giants would uncover further riches.

Jeremy McQuoid
Teaching Pastor, Deeside Christian Fellowship, Aberdeen,
Scotland and Chair of Council, Keswick Ministries

In *Home Safe*, Roger has mined out precious jewels from reformed thinkers before us. And then Roger further shines the Gospel on those jewels so that the beauty of God's grace and Christ's finished work sparkles brightly on every page! I was blessed to be reminded from Scripture of the assurance believers have in Christ. I look forward to using *Home Safe* at home and in the church and seeing God work through it to bring peace and joy to many Christians!

Jathan Newton
Pastor, Abounding Grace Church, Visalia, California

HOME SAFE

A Treasury of Quotes on the Assurance of Salvation

ROGER IBRAHIM

Copyright © Roger Ibrahim 2021

paperback ISBN 978-1-5271-0724-3
ebook ISBN 978-1-5271-0821-9

10 9 8 7 6 5 4 3 2 1

First published in 2021
by
Christian Focus Publications Ltd,
Geanies House, Fearn, Ross-shire,
IV20 1TW, Great Britain.

www.christianfocus.com

Cover and interior design: Rubner Durais

Printed and bound by
Bell & Bain, Glasgow

CONTENTS

Preface 7

Martin Luther 1483 – 1546 11

William Perkins 1558 – 1602 13

Arthur Hildersham 1563 – 1632 15

John Rogers c. 1572 – 1636 17

Bishop Hall 1574 – 1656 19

Richard Sibbes 1577 – 1635 21

Archbishop Usher 1581 – 1656 25

William Greenhill 1591 – 1671 27

Samuel Bolton 1606 – 1654 29

Thomas Brooks 1608 – 1680 31

William Gurnall 1616 – 1679 33

John Durant b. 1620 35

William Guthrie 1620 – 1665 37

John Flavel c. 1627 – 1691 53

Elisha Coles c. 1640 – 1680 55

Thomas Boston 1676 – 1732...57

John Gill 1697 – 1771...61

Archibald W. Alexander 1772 – 1851 65

Thomas Scott 1783 – 1860 69

Charles Hodge 1797 – 1878...71

James Buchanan 1804 – 1870.......................................73

William Cunningham 1805 – 1861...........................75

Horatius Bonar 1808 – 1889 77

Octavius Winslow 1808 – 1878 81

J.C. Ryle 1816 – 1900...85

C.H. Spurgeon 1834 – 1892...105

D.L. Moody 1837 – 1899...109

H.A. Ironside 1876 – 1951..115

A.W. Pink 1886 – 1952...119

John Murray 1898 – 1975 135

PREFACE

'Resolved: Constantly, with the utmost niceness and diligence, and the strictest scrutiny, to be looking into the state of my soul, that I may know whether I have truly an interest in Christ or not; that when I come to die, I may not have any negligence respecting this to repent of.'
—Jonathan Edwards

Speaking to Martha on one occasion, our Lord Jesus Christ said, 'Martha, Martha, you are worried and troubled about many things. But one thing is needed' (Luke 10:41). Perhaps this single divine statement is the key by which we may open the door to eternal life. 'One thing is needed.' How many professing Christians honestly believe this? With the ever increasing upgrades in technological toys and gadgets, with the insatiable urge for wealth and the desire for bigger and better homes, cars, vacations, etc., who does not feel the tug and pull of worldly allurements? As Christians, we are incessantly bombarded with advertisements via the television or Internet that convey the subtle message that somehow our life is not complete or fulfilling without this product, or this vacation, or this experience. While we may intellectually debunk these material onslaughts as 'worldly' or 'extravagant', we must confess that they are formidable temptations to even the most devout Christian that only as he is armed with the full armor of God can he 'not love the world or the things in the world' (1 John 2:15).

More than this, however, the rise of the love and affection for the material and tangible things of this world has imperceptibly buried out of sight and mind what our Lord called, the one thing needful—the salvation of our immortal soul. The more we acquire the superfluous toys of this perishing world and indulge and glut our senses with the passing things of this world, the more we stifle and suppress the vitality and vigor of our spiritual life. The one thing needful becomes the last thing attended to, if attended to at all.

When Christians experience a reawakening of spiritual realities, perhaps the most important question that occupies the mind is: 'Am I a Christian?' Closely followed by, 'How do I know I am a Christian?' To help answer these questions is the purpose of this little book. Thankfully our Christian forefathers wrote amply on this cardinal subject. In my own personal quest to make

my calling and election sure, I have read extensively on the subject. However, as is always the case, I had to wade through many pages before I encountered exceptional quotes that ministered to my own soul. Somehow I wished to remember these 'golden sayings' whenever I began to doubt my salvation again. So I decided to record these quotations by author and number for future reference. Some of the quotes seemed loaded with connotations that I wrote a brief commentary on each for the purpose of elucidation and elaboration only. It evidently began to take the form of a Christian devotional or study that targets one specific theme: The assurance of salvation. The compiling and writing of this small work proved to be an enriching labor and a blessing to my own soul; as such, I thought it might be a source of comfort and blessing to many other souls who are beleaguered with painful questions concerning the state of their own souls. It is never the intention of our compassionate Savior that we wallow in a sea of unbelief and uncertainty concerning our personal interest in Christ. My prayer is that, if it pleases the Lord, other struggling and downcast Christians and seekers would find a beacon of hope and encouragement as they draw spiritual food from the pens of many godly men of the past. To Christ be the glory alone.

Roger Ibrahim

MARTIN LUTHER

1. 'From whence arise thy fears? From Scripture? No; all Scripture is on thy side. Hast thou not fled as a poor sinner to Jesus for refuge? Hast thou acknowledged His divine nature, and His all-sufficient work? And though thou art now tempted to doubt, yet some faith is still fighting against unbelief. These are covenant blessings. Thou art weak, but He keeps thee by His power. Thine enemies are strong—but none of them shall pluck thee out of His hand. Thou art willing to join them, and to depart from the living God, but He has promised to put His fear into thy heart, and thou shalt not depart from Him. He meets with thy doubts, and answers all thy objections in a word; for He hath said, "I will never leave thee nor forsake thee."'

What substance of sweetness, food, comfort and cheer these words convey. All doubt is dealt a deathblow if we consider them carefully. The Bible does not condemn me (because I am already condemned), it is sent to me as a message of hope and reconciliation through Christ. If with my heart I accept all its teaching about Christ the Savior, then I have nothing to fear, though I still struggle and stumble in sin and yet I have inclinations to return to my God in humble confession with a desire to repent. My enemies are powerful, but God defends me, and He will make sure they don't destroy my faith so I will not forsake my God. He will strengthen and remain with me at all times.

WILLIAM PERKINS

2. 'For many a man there is of humble and contrite heart, that serveth God in spirit and truth, yet is not able to say, without great doubtings and waverings, I know and am fully assured that my sins are pardoned. Now shall we say that all such are without faith? God forbid.'

While many hypocrites tend to be presumptuous as to their righteous standing before God, many true Christians fear to act presumptuously. When pressed to it, they will acknowledge their saving interest in the Savior, but may do so hesitatingly, or with reservation. This is mainly due to their ever-increasing knowledge of their sinfulness and unworthiness, not to Christ's power or willingness to save.

ARTHUR HILDERSHAM

3. 'A man may be in the favor of God, in the state of grace, a justified man before God, and yet want [lack] the sensible assurance of his salvation, and of the favor of God in Christ...Nay, I will say more: A man may be in the state of grace and have true justifying faith in Him, and yet be so far of sensible assurance of it in himself, as in his own sense and feeling he may seemed to be assured of the contrary (Job 13:24)...The weakest faith will justify. If thou canst receive Christ and rest upon Him, even with the weakest faith, it will serve thy turn. Take heed thou think not it is the strength of thy faith that justifieth thee. No, no: it is Christ and His perfect righteousness which thy faith receiveth and restest upon it that doth it.'

It is partly because the saints are often assaulted with various temptations, storms, attacks of the devil, allurements from the world, and the remaining corruption of their flesh that frequently pulls them down that they are often doubtful, fearful, and dejected in their spirits. They often see things as Jacob did of old: 'All these things are against me' (Gen. 42:36)! When in reality, all things work together for their good because they are called according to God's purpose and thus love God (Rom. 8:28).

JOHN ROGERS

4. 'If it never proves great, yet weak faith shall save, for it interests us in Christ, and makes Him and all His benefits ours. For it is not the strength of our faith that saves, but the truth of our faith; nor weakness of our faith that condemns, but the want [lack] of faith—for the least faith layeth hold on Christ and so will save us.'

We either have true faith or we don't. We either believe the testimony in the Bible concerning the Lord Jesus Christ or we don't. There is no middle or neutral ground here. If we say I'm not sure Jesus is who He claimed to be, then we are not saved; the weakest, yet true faith in the world will believe that Jesus is indeed the Son of God. True faith clings to this foundational truth. It is a supernatural conviction wrought in the heart by the Holy Spirit. 'No one can say that Jesus is Lord except by the Holy Spirit' (1 Cor. 12:3).

BISHOP HALL

5. '...But now that the virtue and efficacy of this happy work is in the object apprehended by thee, which is the infinite merits and mercy of thy God and Savior, which cannot be abated by your infirmities, thou hast cause to take heart to thyself, and cheerfully to expect His salvation...Understand thy case aright...our hold of Him is feeble and easily loosed; His hold of us is strong and irresistible.'

That's why the saints of God should rejoice always and be always comforted no matter how often and how badly they fail spiritually. God alone must save. The Lord is the Author and Finisher of our faith; it commences with Him and finds its end in Him. Christ is all in all (1 Cor. 15:28). If He doesn't hold us up until the end of our earthly journey, then all is lost. His mercy endures forever, not our faithfulness. We are to simply and steadfastly behold the Lamb of God that takes away the sin of the world (John 1:29).

RICHARD SIBBES

6. 'Little favours come from no small love, but even from the same love that God intends the greatest things to us, and are pledges of it; the godly are more thankful for the least favours than worldly men for the greatest: the affection of the giver enhances the gift.'

> *Do you consider yourself a thankful person? How do you know? True thankfulness that honors God flows from the heart that comprehends that 'every good gift and every perfect gift is from above, coming down from the Father of lights, with whom there is no variation or shadow of turning' (James 1:17). Such a heart not only recognizes the least mercies as mercies, but it also recognizes that these mercies are from the direct hand of a loving Father in heaven. This latter fact sweetens those mercies because they reflect the concern and care of our Father in heaven.*

7. 'Whence we may discern a main difference betwixt a Christian and a carnal man, who is short-spirited, and all for the present; he will have his good here, whereas a saint of God continues still waiting, though all things seem contrary to what he expects. The presence of things to come is such to faith, as it makes it despise the pleasure of sin for a season.'

> *The world is always looking for present pleasures or profits. As a matter of fact, for some people, nothing is worth doing unless there is some personal gain to be reaped. 'What's in it for me?' is an all too common objection we encounter. Such an attitude does not characterize the disciple of Jesus. Here's how the apostle Paul put it: 'I, therefore, the prisoner of the Lord, beseech you to walk worthy of the calling with which you were called' (Eph. 4:1). The new-born soul desires to live in a way that honors God, regardless of personal gain, willing even to bear losses for His name's sake.*

8. 'For our Christian calling, we must know that Christianity is a matter rather of grace than of gifts, of obedience than of parts. Gifts may come from a more common work of the Spirit, they are common to castaways, and are more for others than for ourselves.'

It is easy to confuse the grace of the Spirit with the gifts of the Spirit. Some people will argue thus: 'Surely this preacher is a great man of God; look how eloquent and charismatic he is.' Or, 'God is blessing our pastor, just look how successful he has become.' But such marks are not necessarily the bestowal of God's favor on these individuals, but merely His gifts. If God can give the gift of speech to a beast (Num. 22:21-39), He surely can and does give gifts to the unregenerate as well. 'But the fruit of the Spirit is love, joy, peace, longsuffering, kindness, goodness, faithfulness, gentleness, self-control' (Gal. 5:22), and none but God's children possess these.

ARCHBISHOP USHER

9. [The Holy Spirit] 'shows a man a fullness, and depth, and wisdom, and sufficiency in the Holy Scripture, which is utterly hid from the natural man's eyes. He draws him to the Word with an irresistible force, as the light and lantern, and manna, and sword, which are essential to a safe journey through this world. If the man cannot read, He makes him love to hear. If he cannot hear, He makes him love to meditate. But to the Word the Spirit always leads him.'

The Bible tells us that the natural (unsaved) man receives not the things of the Spirit, neither can he know them...they are foolishness to him (1 Cor. 2:14). This is not the case with the Christian. We see things as we read and study our Bibles. We see spiritual truth, doctrine, and principles throughout the Scriptures. We see the Lord Jesus prefigured in the Old Testament under various types and figures. This is a gift of the Spirit. This spiritual insight is given to the elect of

God only by the illuminating work of the Holy Spirit. What a privilege it is to be enabled to behold the sacred and divine mysteries, which are hidden from most people in this world. Let us be thankful for the indispensable work of the Holy Spirit today.

10. 'Faith is but the espying of Christ as the only means to save, and the reaching out of the heart to lay hold upon Him. God hath spoke the Word, and made the promise to His Son; I believe Him to be the only Savior, and remit my soul to Him to be saved by His mediation.'

Christ is our only hope. Our faith is only as good as the object to which it attaches itself. Technically speaking, faith doesn't save anyone; it is Christ alone who saves. Faith is the instrument by which we receive Christ into our hearts, and since it is the only way by which God ordained that we receive Christ, and it is the pure gift of God, it is indeed a precious faith, 'the faith of God's elect' (Titus 1:1). 'And without faith it is impossible to please Him' (Heb. 11:6). But our eyes should always be fixed on Christ Himself, not our faith.

WILLIAM GREENHILL

11. 'The lowest degree of true faith will do it; as Romans 10:9: "If thou shalt confess with thy mouth the Lord Jesus, and shalt believe in thy heart that God hath raised him from the dead, thou shalt be saved." The thief upon the cross hath not attained to such high degrees of faith: He by one act, and that of a weak faith, was justified and saved (Luke 23:24).'

Is this not a very encouraging word? Believe the record of the gospels. Believe Jesus is the Son of God; believe His words about this life and the world to come; believe that He rose from the dead and is enthroned in glory by the Father's right hand and you are a child of God. Notice, the issue is not to understand everything in the Bible, but believe what you do understand in the Bible. May God grant us such child-like faith today.

SAMUEL BOLTON

12. 'You that can clear this to your own hearts that you have faith, though it be weak, be not discouraged, be not troubled...A spark of fire is as true fire as any in the element of fire...The weakest faith hath as equal a share in God's love as the strongest. We are beloved in Christ, and the least measure of faith makes us members of Christ. The least faith has equal right to the promises as the strongest. And, therefore, let not our souls be discouraged for weakness.'

It's not how much faith we possess or even how strong our faith is; our present concern is whether our faith is genuine or not. Is it the true article? Or is it a misguided or misplaced faith? Is it placed in Christ and His finished atoning work alone, or is it contingent on our personal faithfulness and works? Let us strive to discern the authenticity and simplicity of our trust in a living Savior. Let us make sure that it rests upon our Savior's almighty power and loving-kindness to save.

THOMAS BROOKS

13. 'The feeling of and mourning for the lack of faith, and the earnest and constant desire for it, is an infallible sign of faith.'

It appears that the desire for faith cannot exist in one's heart without a measure of genuine faith already existing there. That might be why the disciples of Christ, who undoubtedly believed in Him, nevertheless asked Him to increase their faith. Therefore, weakness of true faith may be confused with lack of faith. Let us thank God for our little faith and He may grant us greater faith.

14. 'Remember this—until a man comes to be willing to have his spiritual and eternal state to be determined by Scripture, he will never enjoy any settled rest or quiet in his spirit.'

We dare not rest our assurance of faith on the mere affirmation of others—even on true believers. While they may be right in their judgment, nothing but passages from the Bible itself can soothe the soul concerning that nagging doubt about our spiritual state before God. Even a single verse from the Bible that supports our condition is infinitely better than many affirmations.

15. 'He who can say "I am a repenting and believing sinner," he may truly and safely conclude that he shall be saved.'

It is significant that the statement: 'I am a repenting and believing sinner,' is in the present tense. True Christians are always repenting and always believing. It will not do to say that I have repented and believed years ago and consequently there is no need to continually repent and believe. Put another way, repentance and faith are not merely isolated acts in a believer's life; they are an integral part of a Christian's lifestyle.

16. 'He who sees an absolute necessity of the righteousness of Christ to justify him, and to enable him to stand boldly before the throne of God—he is the blessed soul.'

Some of these quotes shine with greater luster on the question of assurance. They are like sparkling gems in a heap of gold. This quote is definitely one of them. The statement is lucid and needs no clarification. Perhaps here a question is more suitable: Is it true of you or are you yet in the bonds of self-righteousness?

WILLIAM GURNALL

17. 'It is not crying out against the devil and declaiming against sin in prayer or discourse, but fighting and mortifying it that God looks chiefly upon...He that will be a soldier of Christ, must persevere until the end of his life in this war against Satan.'

It is vain and useless to denounce sin and evil with our lips alone; just as it is equally useless to praise God and speak well of the Bible if, in conjunction with that profession, there is no sincere endeavor to put off the desires of the flesh and walk in the Spirit. In the same way, many people mistakenly believe that God accepts them because of their militancy against outward sin or evil. The test of our sincerity does not lie here, but it examines our willingness or reluctance to lead a holy life. If there is no willingness to turn from our own personal sin, but we clutch it with no intention of releasing it, then we are still in our sins. 'He who covers his sins will not prosper, but whoever confesses and forsakes them will have mercy' (Prov. 28:13).

18. 'But now when a saint falls, he rises, because when he falls he has a principle of life to cry out to Christ and such an interest in Christ as stirs him up to help: "Lord, save me," said Peter when he began to sink, and presently Christ's hand is put forth; He chides him for his unbelief, but helps him...'

> *If the true believer cries out to Christ when he sins, then it follows that an unbeliever does not do so. This is logical because the Bible says, 'And this is the con-demnation, that the light has come into the world, and men loved darkness rather than light, because their deeds were evil' (John 3:19). Therefore, unbelievers do not willingly come to the Light (Christ). While the Christian still retains a sinful nature, a new nature is also implanted within; therefore, while the flesh may still be inclined to sin, the spirit wages war against it, and so this tension remains in the Christian all through his earthly journey (Gal. 5:17). But the un-believer, 'love darkness rather than light,' which is a completely different condition. Both in flesh and in spirit the unbeliever loves darkness rather than light; this cannot be said of the Christian.*

JOHN DURANT

19. 'Some true believers...hope that Christ will not cast them off, but are not sure that He will take them up.'

This is like the incident in the Bible when Jesus was asleep in the boat as His disciples struggled inside the storm-tossed vessel. Their cry to Him was: 'Teacher, don't you care we are perishing?' (Mark 4:38). On the one hand, they went to Him because they realized He's the only one who could save them; on the other hand, the question, 'don't you care?' indicates a level of doubt. Similarly, some weak Christians hope Christ will save them but aren't sure if He's willing to do so. One method for eradicating all doubt from the heart is to consider Jesus again as He is revealed in the gospels. Look, look, and look at Him again. See Him weep over unrepentant sinners; see Him grieve over His own countrymen as they reject Him; see Him reach out to heal the leper, the blind, the lame; hear Him as He

cries out to the multitude: 'Come to me all you who are weary and burdened, and I will give you rest' (Matt. 11:28). Then ask your soul this question: 'Is it possible that such a compassionate Savior would reject me if I come to Him'? I think you know the answer…never.

WILLIAM GUTHRIE

20. 'Very few have, or seek after a saving interest in the covenant; and many foolishly think they have such a thing without any solid ground (Matt. 7:14). Few find, or walk in, the narrow way.'

How true. All we have to do is observe and ask people. Try this experiment: Choose a network of people outside your church or people that you know are not professing Christians (the bulk of humanity). Ask them what they want most out of life or what their greatest desires are. How many of these people do you think will say: 'To know that I'm truly saved'? I think the results will easily confirm the above statement, don't you? Or simply observe the majority of people and watch what they live for, strive for, hope for, seek for. Is it salvation and assurance of it? Do they live in the narrow way of self-denial and mortification of sin? Are they humbled by their sin? I will let you answer these questions for yourself. May we be found in the narrow way today.

21. 'Not everyone who is in Christ does know that he is in Him (1 John 5:13 implies this).'

Yes. That's why Scripture commands us to make our calling and election sure (2 Pet. 1:10). If every Christian was sure that he or she is a genuine born again believer, then such a Scripture would be superfluous; and there's nothing superfluous in the Bible. Let us search our hearts with diligence so we can rejoice when we discover our election.

22. 'Not all who come to a knowledge of their interest in Christ do attain on equal certainty about it (Mark 9:24).'

'Lord, I believe; help my unbelief!' (Mark 9:24) is found in that reference. It is comforting to know that I may be truly saved by grace but remain sketchy about it in my head. Sometimes the best we can do is make probabilities. For example, after self-examination, we might discern one mark of grace (perhaps it's humility) or we might discern a few (love, joy and peace). In any case, we can at least not pass an 'unsaved' verdict upon our souls. We can see some vestiges of the Spirit's work in us and through us, though we desire more certainty. And, who knows, as we continue to believe, obey, and use the means

of grace (Bible reading, Christian fellowship and
prayer), more certainty might come.

23. 'Everyone who attains a strong persuasion of his interest [in Christ] doesn't always hold there (Ps. 31:22; 77:7).'

Again, we can expect some fluctuation of assurance here. In other words, one day we may 'feel' more saved than another day; that doesn't mean that on that other day we are unsaved, it simply means that, like our faith, our assurance can be strong or weak on any given day. Suppose we had fallen into an un-expected sin on a certain day, would it be surprising or unreasonable that we feel less assured about our salvation then? Probably not. Even David, when he was awakened about his sin with Bathsheba cried out to the Lord to not take His Holy Spirit from him (Ps. 51:11).

24. 'Even everyone who does attain a good knowledge of his interest in Christ cannot answer all objections formally made to the contrary.'

Absolutely. We are certainly not perfect; we certainly continue to sin on a daily basis, hence the need for daily repentance and confession of sin. We must remember the spectrum of sin is wider than many of us think. There are sins of commission and sins of omission.

For example, a man may never commit adultery against his wife, but did he love her as Christ loved the Church and gave Himself for her? The former would be a sin of commission, but the latter, which we are more prone to, is the sin of omission.

25. [The thief on the cross] 'had so much faith in Christ's all sufficiency that he judged a simple remembrance from Christ would supply all his need.'

And that earnest, sincere request by the thief was enough to save him and cause the Savior to look upon him with eyes of mercy. Christ's unforgettable response was: 'Today you will be with me in paradise' (Luke 23:43). Do you desire God to remember you in mercy, though you don't deserve it?

26. 'Where [the Lord] convinces of sin, corruption, and self-emptiness, and makes a man take salvation to heart as the one thing necessary, and sets him to use the means of relief, such work rarely shall be found to fail of a good issue and gracious result.'

We cannot completely neglect the means of grace and simultaneously say we are seriously seeking salvation. This is like a very hungry man that never bothers to search for any food. If we deem the salvation of our souls to be the one thing necessary, surely our lifestyle

will reflect some evidence for it. Do you desire to hear the Word of God?

27. 'The convictions of hypocrites and reprobates are usually confined to some few very gross transgressions.'

Conversely, true Christians mourn and lament secret sins, sins of the heart as well as sins of the mind and body. They are also serious about the regulation of their thought life, to bring it into conformity with the Word of God. Remember, he who commits adultery and he who merely lusts after a woman are in effect guilty of the same sin of adultery, according to Jesus (Matt. 5:28).

28. 'The convictions which hypocrites have, do seldom reach their corruptions, and that body of death which works an aversion to what is good and strongly inclines to what is evil. [Rather] they speak loftily, and with some self-conceit, as to their freedom from corruption.'

The pride of an unregenerate person blinds him to the reality of his spiritual condition. Wholly ignorant of the untouchable holiness of God, whose eyes are too pure to look upon iniquity (Hab. 1:13), he is oblivious to his many failings, weaknesses and sins. Such people fashion an image of God in their mind that is not very different from themselves; so why, they argue, would He not accept them?

29. 'This acting of the heart [faith] on Christ Jesus is not so difficult a thing as conceived: It is a "desire" or "appetite" (Matt. 5:6). "If you will," you're welcome (Rev. 22:17). It is "to look" to the Savior (Is. 45:22); "Open my mouth" (Ps. 81:10).'

> *How wonderful is this. The mere desire for Christ is a divine gift. Naturally we would not desire Him because we would not see our need for Him; Christ remains irrelevant to the wicked because they are not awakened to their great peril due to their sins. '... whose minds the god of this age has blinded, who do not believe, lest the light of the gospel of the glory of Christ, who is the image of God, should shine on them' (2 Cor. 4:4).*

30. 'Man perceiving that God has devised a way of satisfying Divine Justice, and recovering lost man by the incarnation of Christ, he thinks this so good and sure a way, that he absolutely gives up with the law and closes with this device; and this is believing or faith, very opposite to works. This cannot fail to be in all gracious persons, in whom many of the actings [forms] of faith are not to be found.'

> *As a bare minimum, the genuine Christian inevitably recognizes, through painful experience, that he cannot keep the law of God; but, when he hears the good*

news that Jesus Christ came into this world and has indeed kept God's law perfectly on behalf of all who take refuge in Him, he rejoices in this gospel, rests his soul there, and is released from the burden of the law.

31. 'Therefore, I call upon men impartially to examine themselves, and if they find that their heart has closed so with that desire of salvation, and is gone out after Him as precious, that thereupon they conclude a sure and true rest in Jesus Christ, and a good claim and title to the crown, since "he that believeth shall never perish, but have everlasting life" (John 3:16, 36).'

We can therefore pose the following questions to ourselves: Do we believe this good news? Do we believe the record of Scripture concerning Jesus Christ? Do we believe that He came in the flesh, suffered and died in our place on the cross, rose from the dead for our justification, is seated on the right hand of the Majesty on high, and is coming again someday to receive us to Himself? And do we find the Lord Jesus Christ to be increasingly precious to us? If so, then we have everlasting life.

32. 'Hypocrites never close with Christ Jesus in that device and Him alone as sufficient; they still hold fast somewhat of their own, at least to help procure God's favor and salvation; they still retain their former lovers,

imagining they may have Christ with these things equally sharing in their heart.'

> *Two things come to mind here: First, unbelievers or nominal Christians are never content to accept that what Christ has done alone is sufficient for our salvation; no, it may be a part of their scheme of salvation, maybe even an indispensable part of it, but it is insufficient on its own. They insist that other works must be done if we hope to be saved. For example, we must be baptized, we must belong to a certain church, we must live a good and upright life, we must, we must, we must. Such people do not really see Christ as the One thing needful and very precious; if they did, they would count all other works as refuse and cling to Him alone. Secondly, Christ does not reign in their hearts; He does not have first place. First place might go to their position in life, their worth and merit, their pedigree, their heritage, their bloodline, or simply their impeccable reputation. It is never Christ alone.*

33. [Believers] 'have no confidence in the flesh and trusting only in God (Phil. 3:3; Ps. 62:5).'

> *This is true of all Christians. This is the basis for their biblical humility. They finally see, by regeneration, that they have nothing to boast of, but much to be ashamed of. God has opened their spiritual eyes.*

Because of this, they understand that their only hope resides in trusting God and His promises alone for salvation. As a line in a great hymn states: 'Nothing in my hands I bring, simply to your cross I cling.'

34. 'This new principle of life, by the good hand of God, makes the man set himself against every known sin, so far as not to allow peaceable abode to any known darkness (2 Cor. 6:14).'

The wording and qualifications here are critical. Darkness and light cannot coexist. Or can they? In every true Christian two principles or forces exist: The flesh and the Spirit. Thus there is darkness existing alongside the light of the new nature. Unbelievers are all darkness. They know not where they're going; but believers walk in the light because they possess the Light of life. Yet because of their flesh, they still struggle with darkness. But here is the key: they will not live comfortably with the darkness. They hope, they seek, they pray, to somehow rid themselves of it once and for all.

35. [It is well with your soul] 'if you blame yourself and approve the law when you fail.'

If we don't have a sense of the goodness, rightness, and just nature of God's law, something is wrong in our souls. If we find God's demands and commandments are unreasonable or unduly strict or unfair, then our souls are in peril. If we are bent on exonerating ourselves at the expense of God's law by saying things like, 'Why did He make me like this?' or 'It's too high a standard' then we are yet to own up to our natural guilt before God for breaking and flaunting His holy law. We would be just like Adam, when confronted for his disobedience by God shifted the blame on Eve; and in turn, Eve shifted the blame on the serpent. Sincere confession of sin is an indispensable element in the regenerated soul.

36. [It is well with your soul] 'if you can say that you often resolve against sin honestly, and without known guile, and do so resolve the contrary good before the evil break in upon you.'

Our intentions are equally important as our actions. The Lord does not judge us outwardly by our appearance, but inwardly by the state of our souls. How a person thinks is a reflection of who he or she really is. That's why the Bible admonishes us to guard our hearts because out of the heart spring all the vital issues of life. Do we have an aversion to sin? When we do sin, do we feel remorse for breaking God's law and offending a holy God?

37. [It is well with your soul] 'if you can say that you are so far exercised with your failings, as to judge yourself wretched because of such things, and a body of death, which is the root and fountain of these things.'

> *Conversely, if you find yourself covering and hiding your sin, without any inclination to confess or forsake it, then this is an ill sign because you are very comfortable with sin. The new nature cannot abide harmoniously with sin; it fights against it until death. 'He who covers his sins will not prosper, But whoever confesses and forsakes them will have mercy' (Prov. 28:13).*

38. [It is well with your soul] 'if you can say that there is a party within you opposing these evils, which would be at the right way, and, as it were, in its element when it is in God's way.'

> *The new nature is uncomfortable in the presence of sin, though the old nature may prevail in us frequently to commit it. Yet, the new nature resists, protests, and laments the commission of any known sin. Put another way, the new nature is mostly at peace whenever it is conscious that it is in the center of the will of God. Again stated differently, the truly converted person will not commit sin high-handedly or brazenly,*

but always with a holy reservation that things would be otherwise.

39. [We know that we are saved when we] 'quit or renounce all thoughts of help or salvation by our own righteousness, and to agree unto this way which God has found out: It is to value and highly esteem Christ Jesus as the treasure sufficient to enrich poor sinners; and with the heart to believe this record, that there is life enough in Him for men: It is to approve this plan and acquiesce in it as the only way to true happiness: It is to point toward this Mediator, as God holds Him out in the gospel, with a desire to lay the stress of our whole state on Him. This is that which is called faith, believing, receiving (Acts 16:31). This agrees to all the descriptions of justifying faith in the Scripture and will be found in all those who have got the new heart from God, and it will be found in none else.'

> *The righteous will always renounce their own righteousness and cleave only to Christ's righteousness. They recognize Jesus as the only One who can save them; they dare not put their trust in themselves or in anyone else, no matter how holy or how renown. The righteous is willing to risk his soul only on the person and work of Jesus Christ alone for redemption from sin and the gift of eternal life.*

40. 'I say if men do not believe that He is the way, and close not with Him as the only way, they shall die in their sins' (John 8:24).

> *It is as if to say, the Christian intuitively recognizes the Lord Jesus Christ as the only Savior in the whole world, and there is none beside Him. The soul recognizes His infallible credentials as the true Messiah and runs out after Him for help and salvation. My friend, have you found your refuge and only hope in Christ alone?*

41. 'If any man wills he shall be welcome (Rev. 22:17). God excludes none, if they do not exclude themselves.'

> *Otherwise, how can God be just in judging the whole world and condemning sinners who sought refuge in Him? It cannot be. 'Shall not the Judge of all the earth do right?' Abraham asked (Gen. 18:25). Of course He will; he cannot do otherwise. But if sinners hear of the precious Savior and scoff, ridicule and refuse to come, then they have excluded themselves from the gift of eternal life and consequently have no one to blame but themselves. People don't come to Christ because they do not wish to come to Him. 'You refuse to come to me to have life' (John 5:40).*

42. 'The man must not only be persuaded that Christ is the way, but affectionately persuaded of it, loving and

liking the thing, having complacency in it, so that it is all a man's desire (2 Sam. 23:5).'

This is what may separate a true Christian from a nominal one; the former is satisfied and happy with the gospel. He is happy to hear that Jesus is the only way to God; he is happy there is such a Savior and rejoices in the Savior's love to him. On the other hand, there are a countless multitude, it is to be feared, that merely assent to the proposal that Christ is the only way we can be reconciled to the Father, but they don't necessarily find this method delightful; nor is it satisfactory to meet their soul's needs and desires. At the very least, they may accept this truth as a gospel fact but are indifferent to it and find it rather irrelevant to their actual lives.

43. 'It shall not fail on His [God's] part, if thou have a mind for the business, yea, I may say, if by all thou hast ever heard of that matter, thy heart loveth it, thou hast it already performed within thee; so that difficulty is past before thou was aware of it.'

Wonderful news. If we are pleased with God's plan of salvation and gladly yield to it, it is evidence that we possess it. The Father said, 'This is My beloved Son, in whom I am well pleased' (Matt. 3:17). I infer from this that if we are just as well pleased with the beloved Son, then the Father is pleased with us. Is Jesus beloved to your soul?

44. 'Now this cleaving of the heart unto Him, and casting itself upon Him to be saved in His way, is believing.'

Two ideas are contained here: The first is that we must not only be pleased with God's plan of salvation in sending Jesus to redeem us, but secondly, we must also reject any other plan. We have not truly done the first without having simultaneously done the other. Christianity is exclusive; Christ is exclusive. We find Him saying things like, 'I am the good shepherd;' 'I am the light of the world;' 'I am the door;' 'I am the way the truth and the life' (John 10:11; 8:12; 10:7; 14:6). His true followers must recognize His exclusive claims, and they wouldn't have it any other way.

45. 'Remember: That in those to whom the Lord gives the new heart, forming Christ in them, the whole heart is not renewed; there is flesh and spirit lusting against each other, the one contrary unto the other, so that a man can neither do the good or evil he would do with full strength (Gal. 5:17). It is well if there be a good part of the heart going out after Christ, desiring to close with Him on His own terms.'

These are cheering words indeed. Christians fall into sin, sometimes grievously. Frequently they feel the tug and pull of their flesh to follow after the world and do as the world does. This is because of their

yet unredeemed flesh. Still it is a very real struggle that should not be marginalized. Like David, if left to ourselves, we have the potential of committing such heinous crimes like adultery and murder! The seeds of these sins are implanted deep within our fleshly nature, and it is only God's mercy and grace that keeps them from germinating and producing death. But, thank God for His mercy. He will not allow sin to dominate us and destroy our lives. One way He does this is simply by giving us the new nature. The new nature fights the old nature and does not allow it to remain dominant. Only the true Christian can understand this struggle. Thus, even in the midst of sin, the child of God cries out to his Father, 'Lord, help me! Lord, have mercy on me!'

46. 'It is according to Scripture to say unto God, I believe, when much unbelief is in me and the heart is divided in the case "Lord, I believe, help Thou my unbelief" (Mark 9:24).'

Therefore our faith is far from perfect. The disciples truly believed in Jesus, but we find Him (probably again and again) saying to them, 'O you of little faith' (Matt. 8:26). While this reality ought to stir us all up to strengthen our faith, it is also consoling in the sense that a little faith will save us, just like it saved the disciples. It is not faith that saves us, but faith that is linked to the right object, Jesus Christ.

JOHN FLAVEL

47. 'We acknowledge no righteousness but what the obedience and satisfaction of Christ yields to us: His blood, not our faith; His satisfaction, not our believing it, is the matter of justification before God.'

It is something that occurred outside of us in actual space and time that saves us. It is Almighty God acting. It is the external, solitary act of Christ's perfect obedience to His Father's will and His perfect sacrifice on the cross as real historical events that don't involve our participation at all which furnish the ground of our justification. 'Nothing in my hands I bring, simply to thy cross I cling.'

ELISHA COLES

48. 'Cleave to Jesus Christ, and to Him only; and trust not to your holding of Him, but to His holding of you.'

> *I could not hold on to Christ even if I tried with all my might. Such is my utter weakness and impotence. What hope do I have then? Great hope, because He has promised to hold on to me. Listen to His words: 'the one that comes to Me I will by no means cast out' (John 6:37), or '[My sheep] follow me...and they shall never perish; neither shall anyone snatch them out of My hand' (John 10:27-30). My total security in life and in death is in Jesus my risen Lord.*

THOMAS BOSTON

49. 'It is true [that] if the firmness of this union [between Christ and the sinner] depended entirely on the hold the sinner has of Christ by faith, it might be broken; but it depends on the hold that *Christ* has of the sinner by His Spirit, as the nurse has of the babe in her arms.'

This is our resting place. When all else fails, we can rush into our Father's arms knowing He knows all and will take care of all that concerns us. When crossing a busy street, the father knows that it's not the little child's clasp of his hand that will secure him, but his own strong clasp of his child's hand that will secure him. How much more can we rejoice in our Father's almighty hand as we realize that underneath us are the almighty and everlasting arms of God (Deut. 33:27).

50. 'We need no other righteousness for justification but Christ's.'

This becomes increasingly salient as we realize that we have no righteousness of our own. Therefore

Christ's righteousness must be enough, or we have no hope of salvation. Let us guard our hearts against the risings of secret pride. O let us humble ourselves underneath that old rugged cross, where the agonizing Savior cried, 'It is finished!' (John 19:30). Redemption is accomplished. We are saved, not according to our righteousness but according to His mercy (Titus 3:5).

51. [Those united with Christ] 'have given up the law as a covenant of works and betaken themselves wholly to the grace of Christ in the [New] Covenant.'

The newly converted Christian has altering views of good works: First, he perceives that without good works he can never please God; secondly, after many failings, he despairs of his best works to satisfy God's holy standard; thirdly, and only as he understands and rests in Christ's satisfaction for sin, he gladly performs good works because he loves God; he loves God because he has experienced God's love for him. Thus his work is driven and motivated by gratitude for what God has done for him, rather than a means for meriting God's favor.

52. [Those united with Christ] 'have hearts that are separated and disjoined from sin and laboring to take up their everlasting rest in Christ as the center of their desires (Ps. 119:128; 73:25).'

It is not that the Christian no longer has any inclination to sin; this would be a dishonest assessment of his condition. Rather, there is now a certain aversion or distaste for sin that was perhaps previously relished before conversion. Yes, the flesh might still desire it, but the spirit resists it. A new life has invaded the old. New hopes, new desires, new aspirations have suddenly come. If anyone is in Christ, he has become a new creation; the old has passed, but the new has come (2 Cor. 5:17). Do you know anything of this wonderful transformation?

53. [Those united to Christ] 'are carried out of themselves into Jesus Christ (Matt. 16:24).'

The phrase, 'carried out of themselves' is a suitable expression to show that Christians are not redeemed by any inherent worthiness. It is useless to look into our own hearts. Jesus put it simply: Out of the heart proceeds adultery, thievery, murder, etc (Matt. 15:19). No, the Christian realizes that he cannot trust his own heart, for the Bible also says, 'He who trusts in his own heart is a fool' (Prov. 28:26). Thus, we need a living Savior that will save us from ourselves. Thank God, He has provided the Lamb that takes away the sin of the world (John 1:29).

JOHN GILL

54. 'In this new man are new eyes to see with. To some, God does not give eyes to see divine and spiritual things, but to the regenerated ones He does. They have a seeing eye made by the Lord (Deut. 29:4; Prov. 20:12) by which they see their lost state and condition by nature, the exceeding sinfulness of sin, their own inability to make atonement by anything that can be done by them. [They see] the insufficiency of their own righteousness, their impotence to every good work, and lack of strength to help themselves out of the state and condition in which they are. [They see their need] of the blood, righteousness, and sacrifice of Christ, and of salvation by Him. They have the eye of faith by which they behold the glories of Christ's Person, the fullness of His grace, the excellency of His righteousness, the virtue of His blood and sacrifice, and the suitableness and completeness of His salvation. Regeneration, in this view of it, is no other than spiritual light in the understanding.'

As the old hymn goes, 'Once I was blind, but now I see.' This is the experience of every newborn child of God. Before their conversion, they were blind to sin, blind to God, blind to the beauty and glory of Christ, yes, utterly blind to the spiritual and eternal realities which they must shortly see with their own eyes. But believers perceive these things now. No, not with their physical eyes, but through the eyes of faith. They know that soon they must launch into worlds unseen and face the great tribunal of God. Thus they bear testimony of their utter need of Christ and see the preciousness of His Person.

55. 'Moreover, in the new man are new ears to hear with. All have not ears to hear; some have, and they have them from the Lord, and blessed are they (Rev. 2:11; Matt. 13: 16-17)!'

'He who has ears to hear, let him hear' (Matt. 11:15), was a frequent and rather odd expression on our Lord's lips. When we hear it for the first time without thoughtful reflection, we might stumble over its spiritual significance. After all, doesn't everyone have ears? Therefore everyone can hear, right? Sure, most of us can hear with our physical ears, but, as is often the case, Jesus is illustrating a spiritual truth by earthly, tangible things. The ears to which He refers are 'spiritual and invisible' ears. Not everyone has

them. Only those who have received the Holy Spirit and responded to the effectual 'call' of the gospel can truly hear what Jesus is saying. That is, they can accept and have some understanding of His message. Let us ask the Lord to grant us spiritual ears.

56. 'A regenerate man breathes in prayer to God and pants after Him, after more knowledge of Him in Christ, after communion with Him, after discoveries of His love, particularly after pardoning grace and mercy. Sometimes these breathings and desires are only expressed in sighs and groans, yet these are a sign of life. If a man groans, it is plain he is alive.'

What wonderful language of hope is this to the doubting soul. Long and arduous prayers are not necessary to merit or evidence new life. A simple groan after Christ means a man is alive. Unregenerate men have no such groans after God; it is only those that have been awakened from their spiritual death that now grope after the Savior for more love, more light, more knowledge, etc. Do you know anything about this precious token of eternal life? Ask and you shall receive (Matt. 7:7).

57. 'There are, in a regenerated man, cravings after spiritual food, which show that he is made alive...They feel the burden of sin on their consciences, the workings

of the Spirit of God in their heart...A dead man feels nothing. They have a spiritual taste, a gust for spiritual things...They savor the things [that are] of God and not of men.'

Just like all healthy people crave food when they're hungry, the Christian craves 'spiritual manna' from heaven to satisfy his soul. Nothing else will do. Physical food is not enough to satisfy the conscience that is laden with sin. It must feed on that manna, which is Christ Himself to be nourished, strengthened and enlivened. Christ freely offered Himself on the cross as a sacrifice for sin, that Christians might partake of this spiritual feast and find strength for their souls. One look of faith toward the crucified Son of God is enough to impart life to the worn and weary soul. May we look to Him by faith today.

ARCHIBALD W. ALEXANDER

58. 'If believers doubt of their own sincerity, yet they do not and cannot doubt of Christ's excellency and suitableness. His doctrines they humbly receive, and they found their hopes of salvation on His faithful Word alone. The doctrine of Christ is not merely what He taught as a prophet, but it is also the doctrine which respects Himself. Christ Himself is the center, the substance of Christian doctrine. His divinity, His incarnation, His holy life and miraculous works, His sufferings and humiliation, His crucifixion as an atonement for sin, His resurrection and ascension, and His glorification— these truths which relate to Christ's person and work, are known to be divine by everyone who is truly enlightened by the Spirit of God.'

> *One of the marks of genuine faith is a rejoicing in the truth of the Bible. The doctrines of Scripture, like the deity of the Lord Jesus Christ, the sovereignty of God, the overruling providence of God, the love of God,*

and so on, are not concepts that unbelievers find joy-
ful. As a matter of fact, they may find many of these
doctrines like the holiness of God quite dreadful, since
it threatens punishment on the works of darkness.
But believers rejoice in the truth. They are enabled to
rejoice in the truth because the Spirit of Truth resides
in them. This is especially true as they consider Jesus
Christ in all His perfections—they rejoice with joy
unspeakable and full of glory (1 Pet. 1:8).

59. 'He has received an unction which teaches him all these things—that is, a spiritual illumination—so that without the authority of any man or any church, he knows by an internal evidence that these doctrines which relate to Christ, are true, and that they came from God. To know the truth, to embrace it cordially, to love it sincerely, and to be molded to conform to it—this is what constitutes one a true Christian.'

What makes one man believe the truth of the Bible
and another man reject it? Many unbelievers flatter
themselves that they have rejected the Bible as a
book of fables because they have 'matured' in their
intellectual capacity to believe the claims of the Bible.
But the Bible tells us why they reject the truth: It is
due to their spiritual blindness and ignorance. Jesus
called the spiritual leaders of His day, 'blind guides'
(Matt. 23:24). Christians, on the other hand, have

been enlightened by the Holy Spirit so that they not only spiritually see and understand the truth, but also love it.

60. 'Every true believer has the witness in himself. He needs no external evidence to convince him of the truth of the gospel.'

Have you not found it to be so with you? Where does unshakable conviction come from? What would make a person rather die than to deny Jesus Christ? These questions are profitable to meditate on. The martyrs throughout the running generations were no fools. Many of them were highly respected and learned men and women. Yet, they were willing to endure atrocious pain and death rather than deny the truth they dearly loved. How did they do it? Maybe the answer is that they were enabled to look on the things that are unseen (2 Cor. 4:18), and saw the unseen Christ beckoning them to their homeland.

61. '...And he not only sees and believes that Christ is in all respects a suitable Savior, just such a one as he needs, but he sees a divine glory shining in the face of Jesus Christ, by which he is also attracted and his thoughts so occupied that he forgets about himself.'

What do you think of Jesus Christ? This is the question upon which the eternal destiny of every human being

hangs. The true believer has seen glimpses of the glory of God in the face of Jesus Christ. Not that he had witnessed a visible miracle of any kind, but a glimpse of the majesty and glory of Jesus Christ was revealed to his soul. Ever since that moment, he is never the same man. He knows Jesus is real; he knows Jesus is God; he knows Jesus is reigning as King and He will shortly come again to be glorified in His saints.

62. 'This is the divine anointing, which if a man possesses, he needs no one to witness to him that Jesus Christ is the Son of God, and the Savior of the lost.'

It is truly a supernatural event that takes place in the soul, hidden from the naked physical eye. It cannot be rationally explained or understood. It just is. The Christian believes the truth even if he were the only one on earth who does. He knows it to be true, not through debate and intellectual argumentation, but by a divine conviction that these things are so. Jesus said: 'No one can come to me unless the Father who sent Me draws him' (John 6:44). Do you know anything of this relentless magnetic attraction to Christ? If so, rejoice, Christ Jesus is your Savior.

THOMAS SCOTT

63. 'Regeneration may be defined [as] a change wrought by the power of the Holy Spirit in the understanding, will, and affections of a sinner, which is the commencement of a new kind of life, and which gives another direction to his judgment, desires, pursuits, and conduct.'

Thus, the supernatural act of regeneration transforms the whole man in all his faculties. He is renewed in his thinking, he has new desires and aspirations, and his emotions are sanctified. This is what theologians call a new principle. The old sinful nature is still resident within him, but now a new nature has come. Hence the internal conflict, which is existent in every regenerated soul, is born. Practically speaking, therefore, the renewed person cannot feel at home in this present world anymore. '[I] desire to depart and be with Christ which is far better' (Phil. 1:23).

CHARLES HODGE

64. 'God does not pronounce the ungodly to be godly. He declares that notwithstanding his personal sinfulness and unworthiness, he is accepted as righteous on the ground of what Christ has done for him.'

Otherwise there would be no hope for any of us. After all, which of us can say that we have never sinned since our conversion to Christ? None if we are honest. That is why the doctrine of justification by faith alone is so crucial to our proper understanding of salvation. We desperately need a substitute to stand in our place and endure the wrath of God's holy justice against sin, or the divine eye will detect spots of iniquity on us all.

JAMES
BUCHANAN

65. 'Let the sinner close with Christ in His scriptural character, in other words, let him have a correct apprehension of Christ as He is revealed in the Gospel and cordially believe on Him...as his own Savior, in all the fullness of His offices, and he is really from that time a converted man, however defective his knowledge and experience in many other respects may be...This decisive act implies that the man feels himself to be a sinner...while he has no means and no power to save himself, but must be indebted to a Savior...it implies that he is made willing to receive, own, and submit to Christ as God's anointed One...He willingly submits his understanding to Christ's teaching...He willingly acquiesces in the method of being justified, not by his own righteousness but by the righteousness of Christ. [He is willing] to surrender himself unreservedly—soul, body, and spirit—into Christ's hands; to be saved, sanctified, governed, and dealt with now and eternally, according to the terms of the everlasting covenant...But the truth

is either not duly understood or not really believed, where it works no change on the heart and habits of the sinner...'

> *It is difficult to understand how a person can read through the gospel narratives without bias or preconceptions and not fall in love with Jesus Christ. What can we desire more? Here is God, clothed in human flesh, coming to seek out and save a cruel and rebellious humanity. The God-Man reaches out His hand to the lost multitudes and passionately invites them to come to Him that they might find true and everlasting life; that their sins may be forgiven; that they might be reconciled to God the Father; that they may experience joy unspeakable and full of glory in the present life and pleasures forevermore in the life to come. Here is the King of Kings coming to us with a meek and lowly heart, beseeching us to take His hand so He can navigate us safely out of this wilderness which has often deluded us into thinking it's our resting place. Can such a Person be despised by any sound mind? It appears unthinkable. Lord, grant us a sound mind as we encounter You in your Word today.*

WILLIAM CUNNINGHAM

66. 'It is not indeed, then, as a work or a grace that faith saves: It is merely the instrument of uniting us to Christ. His work is the sole ground of our salvation and of all that is connected with it. We owe it all to Him.'

Perhaps there is no sweeter doctrine than this: Jesus did it all; all to Him I owe. Yet it is one of the most misunderstood and maligned doctrines. By nature, people strive to give credit and great worth to themselves, but the all-sufficiency of Christ brings them down into the dust of humiliation. This is incompatible with sinful human pride; therefore it is generally abhorred and rejected in place of a more humanistic approach to a dignified humanity. But it will not stand, for God insists: No flesh will boast in my sight (1 Cor. 1: 29). Let us rather approach God with humility, that He may lift us up in due season (1 Pet. 5:6-7).

67. 'Our faith is that which carries us out of ourselves to Christ, transferring our whole dependence, as it were, from our doing to what He has done and suffered for us. And it is a constant act of trust, a confidence in Him for everything pertaining to another world. It bears at all times upon it a declaration of our utter inability to do anything for ourselves...It is both in form and substance a casting [of] ourselves entirely and unreservedly upon His mercy through Christ and resting upon Him alone. We believe in the Lord Jesus Christ and are saved.'

It is incredible how this simple gospel of genuinely good news is besmirched, beclouded and eclipsed with unnecessary and cumbersome stuff of the flesh. He is God in human flesh. Can He not do everything for us to procure our everlasting salvation? We are dead in trespasses and sins (Eph. 2:1). How can we do anything to make ourselves alive in Christ? No, God must do all or nothing will be done, and we are forever undone. Let us thank God that He did all that is necessary for us to be reconciled to Him in Christ.

HORATIUS BONAR

68. 'Our justification is the direct result of our believing the gospel...Our faith is but our touching Jesus; and what is even this, in reality, but His touching us?'

As we read the gospels and contemplate the majesty of Christ, doubts may sometimes arise as to the reality of this Person. Is He real or merely a figment of someone's imagination? His unique character and powerful (supernatural) life may make us at times wonder if such a Person did ever really exist. However, as we surmount this unbelief by the power of the Holy Spirit and in a moment of time to grasp the reality of the Person of Christ, and subsequently be cheered or consoled by that reality, then Christ has 'touched' us and faith is born in our souls.

69. 'All faith here is imperfect; and our security is this, that it matters not how poor or weak our faith may be: if it touches the perfect One all is well. The touch draws out the virtue that is in Him, and we are saved...So a feeble,

very feeble faith, will connect us with the righteousness of the Son of God; the faith, perhaps, that can only cry, "Lord, I believe; help Thou my unbelief" (Mark 9:24).'

The excessive scrutiny of the genuineness of our faith may be less profitable than the realization of the sufficiency of Christ to save us. For the simple confidence that believes that Christ is who He said He is and did what the biblical record tells us He did is all that is necessary for salvation. But how can we come to that certainty of the biblical record? There is no other way but to diligently read the Scriptures and pray over them. That is our part; God's part is to shine in our hearts to give us the knowledge of God's glory in the face of Jesus Christ (2 Cor. 4:6).

70. '[Faith] listens to the "It is finished!" of the Sin-bearer and says, "Amen." Where faith begins, there labor ends—labor, I mean, "for" life and pardon.'

Paul draws the following conclusion: 'Therefore we conclude that a man is justified by faith apart from the deeds of the law' (Rom. 3:28). Faith, in the first place, is not doing, but believing truth. It observes Christ suffering and dying on the cross for sinners and exclaims: 'That's it! Christ died for me, a sinner. I believe it, I accept, I cherish it. As a matter of fact, it is my only hope if ever I am to be saved.' Note this is

not a work of any kind, but a simple growing confidence that Jesus is the Savior and He died to save me from my sins.

71. 'Faith is rest, not toil. It is the giving up of all the former weary efforts to do or feel something good in order to induce God to love and pardon; and the calm reception of the truth so long rejected, that God is not waiting for any such inducements, but loves and pardons of His own good will and is showing that good will to any sinner that will come to Him on such a footing, casting away his own performances or goodness, and relying implicitly upon the free love of Him who so loved the world that He gave His only begotten Son.'

Two things are imperative for us to understand, if we would have an accurate comprehension of the 'irreducible minimum' requirements for saving faith to be discerned by those who are anxious to know their spiritual state: First, we must have come to the place where we whole-heartedly reject the idea that we have any inherent righteousness that would satisfy God's standard of holiness in any way; secondly, having discerned, felt, or experienced this in our lives, we consequently cast ourselves entirely on the free grace and mercy that Jesus Christ offers to all who will come to Him for it. 'Come to Me, all you who labor

and are heavy-laden, and I will give you rest' (Matt. 11:28-30).

72. 'Faith is the acknowledgement of the entire absence of all goodness in us and the recognition of the cross as the substitute for all the want [lack] on our part...Faith does not believe in itself, but in the Son of God; like the beggar, it receives everything, but gives nothing. It consents to be a debtor forever to the free love of God...It rejoices in another, not in itself; its song is, "not by works of righteousness that we have done, but according to His mercy He saved us" (Titus 3:5).'

> *Because of the seeming simplicity of this way to God, many have stumbled and were offended by the nature of biblical faith. It seems too easy; 'surely', they say, 'God requires more of us than simply to believe the record of the gospel and to rest in Christ. We must do many things to be counted worthy to enter the kingdom of God.' And so the Jews of old asked Jesus, '"What shall we do, that we may work the works of God?" Jesus answered and said to them, "This is the work of God, that you believe in Him whom He sent"' (John 6:28-29).*

OCTAVIUS WINSLOW

73. '"I will arise and go unto my Father" (Luke 15:18) is the first motion of a renewed soul.'

> *Putting it negatively, Christ said to the Jews, 'You are not willing to come to Me that you may have life' (John 5:40). Coming to Christ just as we are is the first and main thing in the Christian life; as a matter of fact, this is not a one-time event for the Christian but rather becomes a habitual thing, day by day, throughout the course of life. Moreover, the Christian is never weary of coming to Christ (even if it involves painfully confessing sin) because he knows this is where he will find forgiveness for his sin, relief for his pain, comfort for his sorrow, peace for his conscience, and strength for his duties. May we come to Christ even now in silent prayer.*

74. 'Trust in a reconciled God and Father was no mark and portion of his unrenewed state. It was then trust in self, in its imagined wisdom, strength, and goodness.'

Before the Holy Spirit renews us, we are like the rich young ruler we read about in the gospels (Luke 18: 18-22). Notice his response to Jesus when he inquired what he must do to inherit the kingdom of God: Jesus said to him you must keep the commandments, but he said I already did, since my youth onward. Incredible. Tragically, the young man had no true concept of sin and the depth of human depravity. If he did, he would not have answered Christ glibly and with such reckless self-confidence. His response betrays a lack of confidence in Christ as the One who can save him and overconfidence in himself as 'Good'—well deserving of heaven just as he is. No, when a person's eyes are opened to see the true nature and defilement of sin, his cry would resonate with Paul's: 'O wretched man that I am! Who will deliver me from this body of death!' (Rom. 7:24).

75. 'Oh, how safe he feels in God's hands and under his government now! His soul, his body, his family, his business, and his cares are completely surrendered, and God is all in all. Reader, this is to be born again.'

Isn't this beautiful. What a wonderful state to be in. God is my Father, He controls everything that may affect me; He promises to work all things out for my ultimate good, so I can gladly cast all my burdens on Him, knowing that He cares for me (Ps. 55:22).

I need not fear anyone or anything because the arm of omnipotence is engaged for me. I can seek my Father's kingdom first, because He promises that all my needs will be met. Why should I be anxious for anything when I know My heavenly Father is on my side? May the Lord increase our faith that we may abandon our all to Him.

76. 'True, he feels a self-righteous principle closely adhering to him all his journey through the wilderness... but in the sober moments of his judgment...the language of his heart is, "Other refuge have I none, hangs my helpless soul on Thee."'

This is increasingly the language of the Christian's soul as he matures in Christ. The more he gets to know Jesus, the more he sees his own insignificance and vileness. The more he sees his own nothingness, the more precious the Savior becomes to him. The more he encounters his own failings and weaknesses, the more he takes refuge in his Father's almighty arms, trusting that God alone can cover his head in the day of battle. May we take refuge in Christ this day.

77. 'That soul never perished that felt itself to be vile and Jesus to be precious.'

If we did not feel our own insufficiency and corruptions, we will neither feel our need for a Savior. No,

the law of God must lead to Christ; that is, God's law must first do its work of condemning us before we can become sensible of our dire need for a Redeemer. The rich young ruler (Mark 10:17-27), in his blindness did not see that the Law condemned him, thus he did not see his need for Christ; on the other hand, the thief on the cross cried, 'Lord, remember me when You come into Your kingdom,' (Luke 23:42)—clearly expressing his need for a Savior. May our confidence grow in our Savior today.

J.C. RYLE

78. [The new man] 'no longer thinks "a little sin" is a trifling matter...As for his daily conduct, he allows himself in no known sin. He makes no compromise with his old habits and his old principles...I do not say but that he comes short and finds his old nature continually opposing him—and this, too, when no eye can see it but his own...He is at war, in reality, with the devil and all his works and strives constantly to be free. And do you call that no change?'

It is a marvelous change indeed. It may not appear so to the poor struggling Christian, but remember that the slightest inclination to draw near to God is nothing short of a work of God. The Bible emphatically tells us 'There is none who seeks after God.... There is none who does good, no, not one' (Rom. 3:11-12). And the highest 'good' is communion with God. It follows then, that if we sincerely seek fellowship with the living God through Jesus Christ, then we have indeed undergone a divine change. Praise God for the least noticeable marks of grace in our lives.

79. 'Look abroad on this world, this evil doing world: Mark how little men generally think about sin and how seldom they judge of it as the Bible does; how easy they suppose the way to heaven—and judge you whether this mark be not exceeding rare...Men may rest assured that until they are convinced of the awful guilt and awful power and the awful consequences of sin, and, being convinced, flee from it and give it up, they are most certainly not born again.'

> *As the saying goes, 'the road to hell is paved with good intentions.' Not only are most people convinced of their own inherent goodness, but also our adversary the devil incessantly deludes them that it is even so. A double chain binds them; they are doubly blind to spiritual realities. Thus they are insensitive to the vileness of sin, and do not see it as a great offense against the most holy God of heaven. But the awakened soul no longer views sin as a trivial inconsequential thing. There is something within that soul that wishes to avoid that sin like avoiding a terminal disease. O may the Lord give us sensitive hearts so we may not sin against Him.*

80. 'Before a man is born of the Spirit, there seems no particular form nor comeliness about the Redeemer...To rest entirely on Him for full and free salvation; to make Jesus, in short, all in all in their hopes of heaven—this is

the most notable mark of all true children of God. They live by faith in Christ: in Christ their happiness is bound up.'

> *Perhaps if we had to reduce Christianity to only one word, that word must be JESUS. The Christian longs for nothing more than to ultimately be with Jesus his Savior. He or she recognizes that to be the ultimate bliss. To finally be home from a weary wilderness where there is no refreshment, to finally be done with sin's power and presence; to finally look into the face of the One who loved him and gave Himself for him, never more to lose His presence or to be separated from his Beloved forever. That is heaven indeed.*

81. 'These are the two first [foundational] marks of the Spirit's work—a deep conviction of sin and forsaking of it and a lively faith in Christ crucified as the only hope of forgiveness...'

> *This is the divine order of a work of salvation. First sin must be viewed as it really is: a transgression of God's holy law. It must be viewed as an awful and dreadful slighting of God's inexorable law that must be visited with the severest punishment—divine wrath. Once a soul is gripped with this view of sin, it is now prepared to gladly receive God's gracious remedy which is the gospel. Now the awakened soul*

eagerly calls for the great Physician to come and heal his soul of the malady of sin. If there is no deep conviction of sin, there is no recognition of danger; if there is no recognition of danger; there is no need for a remedy. If there is no knowledge of the soul's sickness, no physician will be sought.

82. 'He that is born again thinks first about the things that are eternal. He no longer gives up the best of his heart to this perishable world's concerns. He looks on earth as a place of pilgrimage; he looks on heaven as his home...He cares not for the pleasures and amusements of the world around him. He minds not the things of the flesh, but the things of the Spirit.'

The gospel of Christ is so powerful that, when it takes hold of a person it literally and entirely transforms his thinking and perspective on this world. This is no small thing. The Bible states that 'as [a man] thinks in his heart, so is he' (Prov. 23:7). After all, we are the sum of our thought-life. Everything we endeavor to do springs from the inside and so greatly influences our behavior and actions. If this present world is the only thing a person thinks about, if his reflections are confined to this earthly realm alone, how can such a person be a Christian? The hope of eternal life is one of the greatest motivators for the Christian to persevere in trials in this present world. Reader, do you think of

the world to come, or are you only interested in this world?

83. 'What is a natural man? A wretched slave of the opinion of this world. What the world says is right, he follows and approves; what the world says is wrong, he renounces and condemns...Oh, it is a glorious change when a man thinks nothing of the difficulty of confessing Christ before man in the hope that Christ will confess him and own him before the holy angels!'

> *This is true liberty. The true Christian thinks thus within himself: 'God is what matters. If He loves me, it is no great thing if all hate me; if He cares for me, who can harm me? If He provides for my needs, why should I worry? If He accompanies me on my journey, who can compare with His friendship? If He goes before me to prepare my way, why should I dread the future? If He will receive my soul in death, why should I shrink from the Grim Reaper, knowing he is only the conduit to conduct me home. I can sing like the hymn writer of old: 'No one cares for me like Jesus.' O praise His name today.*

84. 'But he that is born again is clothed with humility...He has a deep sense of his own weakness and sinfulness and great fear of a fall. You never hear him professing confidence in himself and boasting of his own attainments—he

is far more ready to doubt about his own salvation altogether...he has no time to find fault in others or be a busybody about his neighbor. It is enough for him to keep up the conflict with his own deceitful [flesh]...no enemy is so bitter to him as his own inbred corruption.'

> *How true this is. When you are born again, you are finally, for the first time, brutally honest with yourself. It's like you see yourself, as you really are, as God sees you, for the very first time. It is the moment of truth. Unbelievers tend to deceive their souls into thinking better of themselves than how God declares them to be in Scripture. This honest assessment of oneself produces the grace of humility. Therefore the Christian is on guard against arrogance and self-conceit. He hates it when he sees it in himself or others—but more so in himself. He realizes that he will not be held accountable for the sins of others, but only his own, so walks humbly, tenderly, even fearfully that he may not offend his Father in heaven. Lord, grant us true humility today.*

85. 'Faith is that poor trembling woman who came behind Jesus in the press and touched the hem of His garment (Mark. 5:27).'

> *So we can say, faith is seeing with new eyes; seeing Jesus, perhaps, as we never saw Him before; seeing*

something in Him that is not found in others. Faith realizes that the person of Christ is special, unique and precious. As a result, like the poor trembling woman, faith moves toward Jesus, it is attracted to Jesus, and perceives that He alone can help—whatever the problem might be. And like the poor woman, that faith which looks to Jesus will never be disappointed.

86. 'Faith is the penitent thief, crying, "Lord, remember me" (Luke 23: 42).'

Uttered from the heart of the despairing, dying thief, these words, nevertheless, reveal true faith in his heart. They reveal true faith because first, they are directed to Jesus; secondly, because they presuppose that Jesus is able to 'remember' and that He is a king going to His kingdom; and thirdly because such words presuppose that Jesus will 'remember' us in mercy when we call out to Him. Have you directed your prayer to Jesus? Do you believe He is the King of kings and the Lord of lords? Did you cry out to Him for mercy, help or remembrance? If so, then you possess true faith. Praise God.

87. 'Faith is Peter's drowning cry as he began to sink, "Lord save me" (Matt. 14:30).'

When you are in any grave trouble or danger, to whom do you go for help first? This is quite helpful

in searching our hearts and discovering where our primary hope and trust is found. Sadly, most of us, in times of distress and danger, seek the help or presence of other earthly mortals around us. They may or may not be able to help us; often they disappoint us. How much better it would be if we could 'set the Lord always before us' and go and tell Jesus first all our troubles, fears, and trials. If we did so, we would soon discover that no matter what the predicament, Jesus will help, Jesus will cheer, Jesus will guide, and thus, we will not be shaken.

88. 'Faith is the anxious, trembling voice, "Lord, I believe, help Thou my unbelief" (Mark. 9:24).'

Therefore, beware that you do not stifle or quench the small stirrings of faith in your heart to believe in Jesus Christ. None of us has 'perfect' faith, and few, if any, begin the journey with Jesus in strong faith. But, feeble, fainting faith in Christ can be strengthened and matured by time and practice. This is a good prayer, after all: 'Lord, I believe, help my unbelief' (Mark 9:24). If we continue to believe, the Lord will help our unbelief.

89. 'Many appear to forget that we are saved and justified as sinners, and only sinners; and that we never can attain to anything higher, if we live to the age of Methuselah.

Redeemed sinners, justified sinners, and renewed sinners doubtless we must be—but sinners, sinners, sinners, always to the last.'

> *Now that's encouraging news. Not that we are sinners, but that the Lord knows we will be sinners for the rest of our days. He knows we're weak, even after believing in Jesus. Moreover, He knows we are weak even after believing in Jesus for many years. If we are honest with ourselves, we ought to confess that we are always weak apart from His strength, yet we can do all things through His strength. Let not any soul, therefore, despair because of sin. Only let us look to Jesus for help, strength and encouragement. He is a compassionate and loving Savior.*

90. 'He must know what it is simply to believe before he can expect to be assured...Happy is the man who really understands justification by faith without the deeds of the law.'

> *Thus here many go astray. Failure to understand that we can never be righteous before the sight of a thrice holy God in ourselves, many like the Jews of old are 'seeking to establish their own righteousness' (Rom. 10:3). But this is futile and will only end in despair and perdition forever, unless we, by the grace of God, apprehend the absolute necessity and reality of*

justification by faith alone. We can never be righteous in and of ourselves. Our righteousness must come from another—Christ alone. It is a foreign righteousness that we must be clothed in if we are ever to behold the Father's smile upon us. And, this imputed righteousness to our account is achieved simply by entrusting our souls wholly upon the Person and work of Jesus Christ.

91. 'There is an inseparable connection between diligence [in growth of grace] and assurance.'

If we want to make gains in our assurance of God's love and acceptance of us, we dare not neglect those divinely appointed means whereby we may obtain greater assurance of salvation. We dare not neglect the reading of and meditation on the Holy Scriptures; we dare not neglect solitary prayer to God in secret where we can unburden ourselves before Him and seek His fresh grace to meet every need; we dare not neglect gathering together with the saints in worship, etc. These are the means or ways that God has provided so we can attain assurance of our salvation. Let us never grow weary or neglectful of them and the peace of Christ will soon be ours.

92. 'It is vain to suppose you will feel assured and persuaded of your own pardon and acceptance with God,

unless you count all God's commandments concerning all things to be right, and hate every sin whether great or small (Ps. 119: 128).'

> *Here is another barometer with which we can examine our spiritual state. How do we feel about sin? Do we categorize sin into 'small sins and big sins'? Do we make allowances for 'small' sins? If this is so, it is not a good sign. When God regenerates our soul, He implants in us a new nature that begins to think, evaluate, and judge things the way God does. We begin to see that all of God's commandments are good, righteous and just; conversely, we begin to see all sin (great or small) as an offense to God, worthy to be punished by eternal death. Is that how we perceive God's commandments? Do we indeed hate sin (in our new nature) and fear it like the plague? If so, this is good evidence of God doing a good work in us.*

93. 'The main thing I urge upon you is this, if you have not got an assured hope of your own acceptance in Christ, resolve this day to seek it. Labor for it. Strive after it. Pray for it. Give the Lord no rest till you know whom you have believed.'

> *Don't just sit there and expect God to strike you with 'lightning', infusing the new nature in you. No, we put ourselves in the right environment and temperament*

to be prepared to receive from God whatever He wishes to give us. Do not misunderstand this. We cannot merit anything from God by employing His appointed means of grace (reading the Bible, praying, etc.), but we are nevertheless expected to do so according to His will. Besides, how else can we show that we are serious and desirous of God's assurance? Is it not by doing the very things He wants us to do?

94. 'You forsake your own mercies when you rest content without it. The things I speak are for your peace. If it is good to be sure in earthly things, how much better is it to be sure in heavenly things? Your salvation is a fixed thing. God knows it. Why should you not seek to know it too?'

It is amazing how we tend to be more diligent and scrupulous over earthly matters than eternal matters. We are inclined to think this present life will go on indefinitely, so we do our best in our business or careers; we plan for our future with our investments, IRAs and retirement. But these things will last only for a little while at best, then we will discover that we're at the door of eternity! Isn't it much wiser, then, to 'seek first the kingdom of God and His righteousness, and all these things [our earthly concerns] shall be added to you' (Matt. 6:33)?

95. 'You must not be surprised if you have occasional doubts after you have got assurance. You are still in the body, and have indwelling sin: The flesh will lust against the spirit to the very end. The leprosy will never be out of the walls of the old house till death takes it down.'

'Now we see in a mirror, dimly' (1 Cor. 13:12). Though we may have a good hope and solid ground for eternal life, we shouldn't be discouraged if we don't 'feel saved' all the time. Seeing in a mirror dimly denotes an imperfect vision at best. We are presently in the world of shadows, as it were, where we see men walking like trees, yet we may still perceive that they are men walking as trees. In the same way, we may not see our title to heaven with 20/20 vision, but we may at least see the outskirts and dim sketches of it. And this will still be a great comfort to us and is worth our every effort to attain it.

96. 'You may know the Spirit to be in a man's heart, by the influence He exercises over his thoughts, affections, opinions, habits and life...Every tree is known by its fruit (Luke 6:44).'

A Christian is one who is in-dwelt by the Holy Spirit. It is impossible for someone who has the Holy Spirit residing in him to be totally uninfluenced by Him. Can God live in a person and be completely ignored?

Impossible. There is conviction of sin; there is sweet communion with Christ; there is an illumination of the mind on spiritual matters. Where do these come from? They come from the gentle prompting of the blessed Holy Spirit of God. Do we know something about that in our daily lives? Those who are devoid of the Spirit understand not the things that He teaches. They are foolishness to them (1 Cor. 2:14).

97. 'Where the Holy Spirit is, there will be a deep conviction of sin, and true repentance for it. It is His special office to convince of sin (John. 16:8). He shows the exceeding holiness of God. He teaches the exceeding corruption and infirmity of our nature. He strips us of our blind self-righteousness. He opens our eyes to our awful guilt, folly, and danger. He fills the heart with sorrow, contrition, and abhorrence for sin, as the abominable thing which God hates.'

The Holy Spirit transforms the mind of a person radically that he adopts God's point of view on everything. He agrees with the Bible that God is transcendentally holy beyond conception; he agrees with the Bible he is a sinner by birth and by choice; he agrees with the Bible that he cannot merit heaven on his own and that he deserves only hell; he agrees with the Bible that sin is a hateful affront against God. In short, he sees himself as a great sinner in need of a great Savior.

98. 'Where the Holy Spirit is, there will be lively faith in Jesus Christ as the only Savior. It is His special office to testify of Christ, to take of the things of Christ and show them to man (John. 15:26)...He points out to the sin-sick soul that we have only to receive Christ, believe in Christ, commit ourselves to Christ—and pardon, peace and life eternal are at once ours.'

> *The chief operation of the Holy Spirit is to disclose Christ to us. He reminds us of the graciousness of Christ, of the love of Christ, and of the utter precious-ness of Christ. He reminds us of the words of Christ to His disciples; of the kindness of Christ on the sick, the blind, the lame, and demon possessed; He reminds us of the patience and submission of Christ under persecution, false accusation, torment, and death. But He also reminds us of Christ's divinity and nobility; of His present exaltation and of His triumphant return.*

99. [The Holy Spirit] 'makes us willing to disclaim all merit of our own, and to venture all on Jesus—looking to nothing—resting on nothing—trusting in nothing but Christ-Christ-Christ—delivered for our offences, and raised again for our justification.'

> *The fact that true biblical Christianity is about a Person, Christ the Lord, makes it unique among all the religions of the world. All other religions render*

obeisance to some nebulous deity that must be ap-
peased by rituals, sacrifices, various works and rites.
But Christianity is about Christ, not a system of reli-
gion which purports to be the way to merit acceptance
with 'God.' Therefore we seek a relationship with the
God who became man, not a religion whereby we can
merit acceptance with God. Therefore we look into the
face of Christ and are saved. Where do we look? In
the gospels, of course, where the Son of Man's life and
words are preserved for all to behold and admire.

100. 'Where the Holy Spirit is there will always be holiness of life and conversation. He is the Spirit of holiness (Rom. 1:4). He makes a man delight in the law of God. He makes a man turn his face toward God, and desire above all things to please Him, and turn his back on the fashion of this world, and no longer make that fashion his god.'

How else can we demonstrate our seriousness with
God? If we are constantly hankering after the world
and the things the world can afford us and are not
striving to mortify all ungodly lust and desires, then
are we not a replica of the unredeemed? No, the
Scripture exhorts us to flee youthful lusts which war
against the soul (2 Tim. 2:22); to seek those things
that are above and not on the earth (Col. 3:1); to not
love the world or the things of the world (1 John 2:15);
to separate ourselves from the world (2 Cor. 6:17).

This is doing business with God honestly, and He demands nothing less.

101. [The Holy Spirit] 'sows in a man's heart the blessed seeds of love, joy, meekness, gentleness, goodness, faith, temperance.'

The blessed Spirit manifests these fruits in the children of God. The fruit does not reach perfection in this life, and often ebbs and flow in a redeemed heart, but never disappears altogether. Our Lord said, 'You will know them by their fruit' and a 'tree is known by its fruit as to what kind it is.' Indeed, He goes further and says a good tree does not bring forth corrupt fruit and an evil tree does not bring forth good fruit (Matt. 7:15-20). Let's prayerfully and soberly examine the fruit we are producing.

102. 'Where the Holy Spirit is, there will always be the habit of earnest private prayer...He makes a man feel he must cry to God, and speak to God, —feebly, falteringly, weakly, it may be, but cry he must about his soul.'

If we don't pray we are not Christians, simply put. It is not that prayer makes us Christians, but rather true Christians pray. As our text points out, our prayer may be as faint as a sigh, but bless God, He counts it a prayer. Now praying before others that can see us pray does not count. This is because even a

hypocrite likes to appear holy in front of other people. The Christian, however, realizes that God reads our hearts, and thus never wishes to fake his devotion, but wishes to be known as sincere before this Holy God, before whom all things are as naked in His sight (Heb. 4:13).

103. 'Where the Holy Spirit is, there will always be love and reverence for God's Word.'

In all true believers, there is an implicit trust in the Bible as the infallible Word of God. They may not understand many things in the Bible; nevertheless, they remain firm on this point with inflexible conviction. This recognition of the Bible's divine origin and absolute veracity springs not out of their own hearts, but it is another fruit of the Spirit that enables them to hold on to the Bible as divine truth as well as cultivate a growing love for it. Some have even given their lives to defend its doctrines. May we read, study, obey, and defend this treasure we hold in our hands.

104. 'The true Christian is counted righteous for the sake of Jesus Christ, the Son of God. He is justified because of the death and atonement of Christ. He has peace because "Christ died for his sins according to the Scriptures."'

Note how everything with respect to our redemption depends on the Person and work of Jesus Christ. His

Person justifies because He is God manifested in the flesh. His work on the cross justifies us because as God manifested in the flesh, it is of infinite value and efficacy. We have peace with God through Christ because His sacrificial death on our behalf is the only thing that can please the Father and assuage a tormenting conscience.

C.H. SPURGEON

105. 'Scripture does not only tell us that man is dead in sin: It tells us something worse than this, namely, that he is utterly and entirely averse to everything that is good and right. "The carnal mind is enmity against God, for it is not subject to the law of God, neither indeed can be" (Rom. 8:7)...His will is desperately set against everything that is right.'

'Rules were meant to be broken.' Have you ever wondered where that expression came from? It springs out of a rebellious un-renewed heart. This is how we all react to rules or restrictions by nature. We undermine them; we complain about them; we seek loopholes around them; in short we break them; if not literally, then spiritually, because we are not submissive to them. One of the marks of regeneration is 'lawfulness.' The Christian no longer seeks to break God's commandments or any other regulation established by a legitimate authority. On the contrary, the

Christian is eager to give 'to Caesar the things that are Caesar's, and to God the things that are God's' (Matt. 22:21).

106. 'It was nothing to you that Jesus should die...you only regarded it as a tale, perhaps even an idle tale...But ah, my hearer, Christ's dying is nothing to thee unless thou hast a living Spirit within thee.'

Now the death of Christ is nothing short than eternal life to the child of God. The true believer recognizes the utter necessity for Christ's death; not only is it not an irrelevant story, but it is the most important event he can imagine. Without Christ's sacrifice on the cross, he is undone; he is ruined, damned forever to all eternity. And in this life he would be condemned to an existence of being separated from God and without hope in the world (Eph. 2:12). That is a dismal state indeed. But thanks be to God, because 'there is therefore now no condemnation for those who are in Christ Jesus' (Rom. 8:1).

107. 'David knew where to obtain full assurance. He goes at once to God in prayer. He knows that knee-work is that by which faith is increased, and there, in his closet, he crieth out to the Most High, "Say unto my soul, I am thy salvation." O my brethren, we must be much alone with God, if we would have a clear sense of His love! Let your

cries cease, and your eyes will grow dim. Much in prayer, much in heaven; slow in prayer, slow in progress.'

> *It is astonishing how deficient most Christians are in prayer. We simply don't pray as we should; we don't read or study the Bible as we should. How, then, do we expect to gain assurance of our salvation? It is imperative that we use God's ordained means to procure insight into our spiritual state. There is no other way we can gain confidence that we belong to Christ and Christ belongs to us than to listen to God's Word and then plead God's promises at the throne of grace.*

108. '...Lord, I have sinned; I deserve it not; I am sinful; I scarcely dare to ask it; but Oh! Say it to my soul, "I am thy salvation." Let me have a pointed, personal, infallible, indisputable sense that I am thine, and that Thou art mine.'

> *Isn't that the great hope and desire of the doubting Christian? How often such a weak believer would sigh, 'O if I only knew for sure that my account is forever settled in heaven; if I only knew for certain that the Lord Jesus Christ loves me, I would be the happiest person on earth!' Yes, the love of Christ is the greatest treasure any human soul can possess, and it is said of Jesus, 'having loved His own who were in the world, He loved them until the end' (John 13:1).*

109. 'The substance of which is just this, when you can take the Word and find that you are the character there spoken of...God is thy salvation.'

> *The Bible says we love Christ, not because we initiate that love, but because Christ loved us first (1 John 4:19). This apprehension of the love of Christ for us is the cause of our love to Him. As a result, we can ask a simple question: My soul, do you love the Savior? The question is not do I love Him perfectly, but do I love Him at all? If the answer to that question is yes (no matter how weak my love might be), I can rest assured that the Savior loves me.*

110. 'I know this day I have no other trust but in the cross of Christ; therefore, I am saved; if you are resting on Christ alone, there is not an "if" or a "but" about it; you are saved. Oh! Do enjoy that thought, and go home and live upon it; it shall be marrow and fatness to your spirit.'

> *Conversely, it is an ill token if my trust is placed on anything or anyone else for my salvation. Jesus assures us that He is the only way to God. He emphatically says, 'No one comes to the Father except through Me' (John 14:6). If I perceive that truth with my soul, if I acquiesce to that truth with my mind and will, and if I love that truth with my heart, then I am indeed resting on Christ alone for my salvation. May it please the Lord to give us such faith today.*

D.L. MOODY

111. 'Now, the difference between a Christian and one that is not a Christian is that the Christian confesses his sins, and the other does not. The true believer will go right to the Lord Jesus Christ and confess his sins. There was a time that I could sin and it didn't hurt me. If I did the same thing I once did it would break my heart. I could not do it. What we want is to go to the Master and tell it all to Him. "He is faithful and just to forgive."'

'If we confess our sins, He is faithful and just to forgive us our sins and to cleanse us from all unrighteousness' (1 John 1:9). We must tell Jesus all that troubles us; our personal sin would be included in those troubles. But how can we tell Jesus about our sin if we don't know Him? We start by reading the gospels and praying in a spirit of faith, believing He sees and hears us. Then, we simply tell Him all about our sin.

112. 'Just square up the account every night before you go to bed. If you have done wrong confess it, and ask God to forgive you, and He will put it away. He delights in

forgiveness. When we do wrong, we want to take our sins right to Him, confess them, and believe that He has put them away.'

Why wait? It will only prolong the estrangement of our relationship with Jesus. It is like having an open, bleeding wound and waiting for a convenient time to treat and bandage it. No, it is best to treat it right away before it festers and grows into something worse. So it is with our sin. If we delay to confess to Christ, it will only aggravate our condition and cause us to sin more.

113. 'So when the Devil comes and says you are not a Christian, tell him the Lord Jesus says you are. He that believeth on the Son hath everlasting life.'

When we merely look to Christ as the Savior who was sent into this world to save sinners and place our hope and trust in Him, we are saved.

114. 'John's gospel is the great one. Believe, believe, believe, he says. That idea is ever before him. Every chapter but two in his writings mentions it. God doesn't tell you to feel; many say they don't feel right to come to Christ. God tells you to believe. You must trust Him first. You must have faith in Him before you can have Christian experience.'

This is designed to give believers comfort. Many times we may have very cold and even strange and mixed

feelings about spiritual things, but if we find that at the bottom of it all we still believe and trust Jesus as the Savior of sinners, all is well.

115. 'We must be able to forgive others before God will forgive us.'

It is not that our forgiving others is the basis for God forgiving us, but rather, one proof that God has forgiven us is our willingness to forgive others for Jesus' sake.

116. 'The moment we are willing to come to Him with our sins He will receive us. He will forgive and heal whoever brings his soul to Him.'

When we see Christ as the great Physician of souls, and recognize our sin as the deadly disease that only He can heal, the rest follows naturally: we simply come to Him for help.

117. 'Now, if you can prove that you are a sinner, this invitation from Christ applies to you ("Come unto Me, all you who are weary and burdened, and I will give you rest"—Matt. 11:28). Don't try to prove your worthiness but your unworthiness. If you want rest come to Christ. It can't be obtained in the world. You can't buy it; your friends can't give it to you; God doesn't call you without

giving you the means of winning it; you can come if you will. Oh, may God give you the power today!'

> One of the most precious facets of the gospel is that 'while we were still sinners, Christ died for us' (Rom. 5:8). Jesus doesn't wait until we are good enough to extend His salvation; He extends His hand to us while we are still in the deepest mire of sin. If we look to Him for salvation, He will reach down and pull us out. God doesn't show us mercy because we are good, but because He is good.

118. 'If we could only save ourselves by our own strength there would be no need of a Savior. The worst enemy man has is himself. His pride and self-confidence often ruin him. They keep him from trusting to the arms of a loving Savior.'

> Jesus told the religious Jews of His day, 'You are not willing to come to Me to have life' (John 5:40). Why not? Apparently it is because they believed they already possessed eternal life; that is, they were fine just as they are, and had no need of a Savior. This perhaps is the saddest condition of all.

119. 'I have great hopes that a man may be saved when he will stop and listen. People are so engrossed with the affairs of this world that but few find time to stop. It is all rush and hurry, and they don't think about their souls.'

It seems the devil has gained great success using this device against us since God created man. He fills our thoughts exclusively with this world and how we are doing in it, that it looms before us as the thing of greatest importance. 'Secure as much as possible from this world; enjoy as much as possible from this world; find your greatest satisfaction in this world,' he is constantly whispering in our ears. There will always be time enough to repent and make things right between you and God when you're old and gray and had your fill of this world, or so the lie goes. But what he won't tell us is that our time is very short in this world, after all; that we intuitively know. How short? That we don't know. It may be shorter than we think.

120. 'So Christ is calling the world to come, but the trouble is they do not heed and won't go.'

Spiritual things always seem to be less real and more remote than material things. We tend to gravitate toward those things we can see and feel. But to the eyes that have been opened by grace, the reverse becomes increasingly true. 'We do not look at the things which are seen, but at the things which are not seen. For the things which are seen are temporary, but the things which are not seen are eternal' (2 Cor. 4:18).

121. 'All you have to do is to show that you want help from God, and He will give it.'

> That's it. 'Ask and it will be given to you; seek and you will find; knock and the door will be opened to you' (Matt. 7:7). It is strange that most people will not leap at such a gracious offer. For unbelief says: This is too good to be true.

H.A.
IRONSIDE

122. 'Faith is just saying 'amen' to what God has made known in His Word.'

> *If you find yourself saying 'Amen' spontaneously to Scripture, whether it is read in the Bible or preached from the pulpit or taught on radio or the Internet, it is the manifestation of faith. It is your renewed spirit concurring with what the Holy Spirit has declared in His Word. Unbelievers may give assent to certain Bible truth, but I doubt they do so with a jubilant 'Amen!'*

123. 'Henceforth, however conscious I may be of daily failure, I find the supreme desire of my heart is to do as He would have me. The regenerate man longs to do those things that please his Lord.'

> *This is natural. Just like the young child desires to please his earthly parent, so the child of God has an inborn desire to please his heavenly Father. What kind of Christian is it that has absolutely no desire to*

please God? Even the world can see the inconsistency of that. If we love only the things the world loves: The lust of the eyes, the lust of the flesh, and the pride of life (1 John 2:16), how are we any different from it?

124. 'But how do I know that He has given the Spirit to me? The answer is that it is the Spirit who bears witness to the eternal verities of the Gospel.'

This is the saying 'Amen' again to the truth of Scripture. The unwavering conviction that the Bible is indeed the Word of the living God, and the way certain biblical passages grip our hearts and leave a lasting impression on our minds is unquestionably the work of the Spirit. True Christians hold certain convictions to be true and unalterable, like, for instance, the deity of Christ, the inspiration of Scripture, and the Triune Godhead to name a few. Are you a true Christian?

125. 'So long as a man considers himself worthy there is no salvation for him.'

This is perhaps another gem. When we truly understand our fallen nature, which we were born with, it should generate a spirit of humility and contrition in us. When we grasp that while we were yet sinners, Christ loved us and died for us (Rom. 5:8), it ought to foster a low esteem of ourselves and a high esteem for Christ and His love. When we finally and clearly see

ourselves as we really are, as the Bible says we are it will humble us before God if we are Christians. Question: Do you consider yourself a humble person? In what ways can you see the spirit of humility evident in your life?

126. 'No one will ever be saved who is not in earnest. The great majority of people drift aimlessly and carelessly on, intent only on gratifying their carnal and worldly desires.'

Are you one of these people we meet everyday just drifting carelessly and aimlessly on through life? Such people have only high aspirations for earthly attainments: more money, more fun, more strokes for carnal pride and lusts. God is not in any of their thoughts. Much less is a holy God (the true God!) in any of their thoughts. If they never think about God, how can they be serious about their salvation?

127. 'He that would be saved must arouse himself to the supreme importance of spiritual things. He must put first things first. In this sense he strives to enter in at the strait gate.'

In contrast with the previous quote, the true Christian has his priorities in the right order. He understands that spiritual things take precedence over earthly things. He sees that spiritual things are eternal, but

earthly things are temporary at best. He strives to bring his life in conformity with his beliefs. He doesn't only say these things; he feels these things; he ponders these things; he desires to live out these priorities.

A.W. PINK

128. 'What alterations are there in our faith! What mingling of unbelief at all times! Is this a foundation to build our justification upon? Abraham's faith, dear reader, was nothing more and nothing else than the renunciation of all virtue and strength in himself, and a hanging in child-like trust upon God for what He was able and willing to do...It was the acting of a soul which found its life, its hope, its all in the Lord Himself.'

> In the beginning of our Christian experience confidence in the flesh and our natural abilities remain strong. As we mature in Christ, however, and we discover to our dismay how often we fail in keeping the way of righteousness, we learn that we cannot lean on this 'broken reed' any longer but we must look to God alone to supply all our needs. In all respects, we can echo John the Baptist's words: 'He must increase, but I must decrease' (John 3:30).

129. 'Justifying faith is a looking away from self, a renouncing of my own righteousness, a laying hold of

Christ. Justifying faith consists first, of a knowledge and belief of the truth revealed in Scripture thereon; second, in an abandonment of all pretense, claim or confidence in our own righteousness; third, in a trust in and reliance upon the righteousness of Christ, laying hold of the blessing which He purchased for us. It is the heart's approval and approbation of the method of justification proposed in the Gospel: By Christ alone, proceeding from the pure grace of God, and excluding all human merits. "In the Lord have I righteousness and strength" (Isa. 45:24).'

> *In other words, to examine ourselves to find out if we truly possess justifying faith, three important questions should be asked: First, do we have adequate knowledge of the gospel and believe it? Second, do we completely reject the idea that we can somehow earn salvation by our own efforts and inherent goodness? Third, do we entrust our souls entirely and implicitly to Christ, relying only on His sacrifice for us on the cross for our salvation? 'No man comes to the Father except through Me' (John 14:6).*

130. 'Only as God supernaturally enlightens is any soul made conscious of the awful spiritual darkness in which it naturally dwells (1 Cor. 2:14).'

> *Without this divine enlightenment, most people are inclined to think rather well of themselves. We are*

all too proud by nature, and are dreadfully averse to think of ourselves as 'bad' people. Our present culture, of course, is partly responsible for shaping our self-perception as good people who deserve the best that life can offer; but our darkened mind quickly grasps this perception because it wishes to escape painful introspection and desires to feel good about itself. But when God shines His search-light on our souls, we are humbled by the discovery of our sins and begin to think of ourselves more biblically and more soberly.

131. 'The principal device of Satan is to deceive people in imagining that they can successfully combine the world with God, allow the flesh while pretending to the Spirit, and thus "make the best of both worlds." But Christ has emphatically declared that "no man can serve two masters" (Matt. 6:24).'

Allegedly, it was Martin Luther who, after being accused of antinomianism (opposed to God's Law), who said, 'We are justified by Faith alone; but that faith is not alone.' Therefore Luther was not preaching antinomianism, but was rather making a distinction between justification and sanctification. Our efforts to please God, then, are not the cause of our justification, but rather the evidence of it. While we cannot separate the two, strictly speaking, we stand justified

solely on the basis of Christ's finished work on the cross on our behalf. Nevertheless, our great enemy seeks to persuade the unwary that, since no Christian can attain perfect holiness in this life, then it is ok to indulge our sinful nature. Here we must be on our guard and inquire diligently as to our motives: Do we truly love Christ that we are desirous to keep His commandments, or are we merely interested in His benefits only?

132. 'None can enter the spiritual realm unless he has a spiritual nature, which alone gives him an appetite for and capacity to enjoy the thing pertaining to it. This, the natural man has not. So far from it, he cannot so much as "discern" them (1 Cor. 2:14). He has no love for them nor desire after them (John 3:19). Nor can he desire them, for his will is enslaved by the lusts of the flesh (Eph. 2:2-3).'

'But the natural man does not receive the things of the Spirit of God, for they are foolishness to him; nor can he know them, because they are spiritually discerned' (1 Cor. 2:14). Perhaps more than any other Scripture, this statement has ministered to many in times of doubt over the condition of the soul. Two things should be noted for our comfort: First, the unregenerate man does not accept as realities the things revealed in the Bible by the Spirit. He may assent to them, but he does not truly believe them to the point of making any

substantial change in his life. For example, if a man knew that a certain medication was necessary to sustain his life, he would make every effort not to miss a dose, because he earnestly believes this. But if he takes a nonchalant attitude about whether or not to take the medication, one must question the sincerity of his faith in the medication. The same is true in the spiritual realm. Secondly, not only does the unregenerate man make light of eternal verities as 'foolishness', but he can't even understand them, because 'they are spiritually discerned'—that is, only the Holy Spirit can illuminate his mind to grasp the truth contained in the Bible. Which of these two characters do you identify with?

133. 'How many a Satan-harassed believer is exclaiming, I greatly fear that I cannot be among the saved, for if I were, I surely would not sin as I do. In view of the raging of my lusts, the frequency of which they overcome my every effort to resist them, it would be presumptuous to affirm that the reigning power of sin was dethroned within me. My friend, David cried, "iniquities prevail against me" (Ps. 65:3). But you say, my heart is such a sink of iniquity, I dare not claim to be regenerated; often I do not loathe sin nor even desire to. Ah, but it is not always thus: are not such seasons followed by contrition and confession!? Yes, you say, but right after I fall again

into the mire, sometimes deeper than before; Ah, but do you stay there? Do you completely abandon the throne of grace? Does not a cry of distress go up from you to God? Then continue crying "Lord, I believe, help Thou my unbelief."'

Is there any reason for the doubting soul to remain in that state? How many of the godliest and noblest servants of God have grievously fallen into sin? Noah gets intoxicated, David commits adultery and follows it up with murder; Abraham lies; Isaac lies; Job succumbs to self-righteousness; Samson disobeys his parents; Peter denies Christ; Peter falls into hypocrisy, and on and on. Yet all these are eminent servants of the Most High who stood by faith alone and are greatly esteemed and beloved by God. So why can't we be numbered with them?

134. 'Oftentimes there is little for the eye of sense to distinguish in those in whom the Spirit dwells from the moral and respectable worldlings; yea, often they put us to shame...but the heart is washed from the prevailing love of sin by the tears of repentance that the Christian is moved to shed frequently. Every new act of faith upon the cleansing blood of Christ carries forward the work of experimental sanctification to a further degree...'

Ironically and unfortunately, sometimes unbelievers may be morally upright even beyond the level of many common Christians. This is a shameful thing of course. They may even be more sharp-sighted to detect sinful blemishes in the character of many Christians. This is indeed sad. But, there is a hidden region unbelievers cannot see: The repentant heart of the Christian. This is the secret chamber, which only divine eyes may pierce into. The Lord sees the secret sighs, cries, and the feeble yet faithful endeavors of believers to live the Christian life. The merely moral person has no interest in that.

135. 'Unbelief remains in the hearts even of the regenerate. Though God imparts to them the gift of faith, He removes not (in this life) the root of unbelief.'

This fact can come frequently as a startling surprise to the Christian. Here we are, saved by grace, cleansed from the penalty of sin as well as its indwelling dominion, but suddenly, we fall into a serious transgression. What now? We must do two things: First, we must realize that the seed of every corruption remains in us. That is, left to ourselves, we are capable of committing the greatest and vilest evils. This is extremely important to know so that we don't fall into morbid depression or despair. But then secondly, we go to Jesus. Yes, we go to Him again, and again, and again.

We go to Him with our sin, calling it what it is, asking for forgiveness and cleansing, and moving forward in our Christian walk. 'If we confess our sins, he is faithful and just to forgive us our sins, and to cleanse us from all unrighteousness' (1 John 1:9). If instead we wallow endlessly over our failure, it is evident we have not understood our nature correctly.

136. 'Unbelief is the *great burden* of the saint.'

Like the great apostle Peter, we often overestimate the strength of our faith. As our Lord announced His impending death on the cross and how all His disciples would subsequently abandon Him and flee for their lives, Peter was first to interrupt with the hasty words: 'Not me Lord! Even if all the others abandon you in your hour of trial, I will not' (see Mark 14:29). But sadly, and probably with great consternation, Peter denies that he even knows Jesus. Why? He had not yet realized his own weakness of faith.

137. 'It is not until God has communicated faith that any soul is *conscious of* its unbelief!—A living faith is necessary in order to recognize our dead unbelief.'

There is a silver lining in a believer's unbelief. He recognizes it. Unbelievers are not sensible of the ebb and flow of faith because they have none. Only believers are sensitive to the waning of their faith

because faith exists in their heart already. Today, if your faith fails, it is appropriate to lament your weakness, but don't stay there. Rejoice that you have faith, even as small as a grain of mustard seed.

138. 'In your unregenerate days you were never *exercised* over your unbelief.'

That's why sinners outside of Christ can sin shame-lessly, boldly, and increasingly. If it feels good or right they pursue it with all their hearts. Why not? There is no new principle to check them, to alarm them, to pro-duce in them the 'fear of the Lord.' While the Christian can and does fall into sin, he cannot do so impudently, brazenly, or high-handedly, as if defying the great God in heaven. No, he cries out like that father of old, 'I do believe, help my unbelief' (Mark 9:24).

139. 'A true Christian does not cloak or excuse his unbe-lief, but honestly acknowledges it before God.'

One of the marks of true faith is not only recognizing sin as sin, but also calling it such. Unbelievers sugar coat sin under the guise of numerous euphemisms. Sometimes they call it mental illness, sometimes illicit affairs, sometimes alcoholism, but never as filthy vile sin, a transgression of the law of God. Even if some are willing to acknowledge it as sin, it doesn't make them shudder that it is committed against the most

holy God in heaven. They love their sin too much to go that far.

140. 'Ah, my reader, if you are not plagued with and burdened by unbelief, if you do not humbly confess the same ['Lord I believe; help Thou my unbelief!'] to God and seek His help about it, then you are of all men most miserable.'

> *The fiercest battles the Christian encounters are those within the heart as opposed to external battles. The battle against sin is in the mind, way before it is manifested outwardly. This is where the struggle for conquest begins and ends. For example, a temptation seizes the mind; the struggle commences whether to yield to the unbelief or to believe God. If unbelief triumphs, the Christian succumbs to a sinful act or behavior; if faith triumphs, he believes God, acts according to His revealed will and demonstrates obedience. Therefore, let us guard our mind, for out of it come the issues of life (Prov. 4:23). O may the Lord increase our faith today.*

141. 'No unbeliever ever shed tears over his unbelief; no empty professor ever groaned because of his questioning of God; no hypocrite is burdened by his doubts and fears.'

Unbelievers are described in the Bible as 'dead in tres-
passes and sins' (Eph. 2:1). Just as a physically dead
person is insensible to pain, a spiritually dead person
is insensible to sin. They drink iniquity like water (Job
15:16). They may occasionally feel the pangs of con-
science after committing heinous sin, but it is quickly
suppressed and buried in oblivion. It is too painful to
think about and may diminish the so-called pleasure
of sin, so it is willingly suppressed and forgotten.

142. 'To the very end of your earthly pilgrimage, you will
be (in yourself) a vile sinner, unworthy of the least of His
mercies.'

Can you, dear reader, acknowledge this? If you can,
thank God He has opened your eyes to see yourself as
you truly are: a sinner saved by grace. It was John
Newton who penned the following words after real-
izing the truth about himself: 'Amazing grace, how
sweet the sound that saved a wretch like me; I once
was lost, but now am found, was blind, but now I see.'
I see that I am a great sinner; but I also see that Jesus
is a greater Savior.

143. 'It is just at this very point that the Christian is
distinguished from the hypocrite: The former humbles
himself and takes his place before God in the dust, ac-
knowledging his wicked unbelief.'

The unbeliever has never experienced true humility. He is proud through and through; he is so proud that he cannot discern pride in his heart, though he can detect the least semblance of pride in another's conduct. Do you know anything about godly humility? It is the moment of truth; it is the moment where the façade is stripped away, false imaginations banished, fantasies concerning oneself repudiated as lies. It is when a Christian views himself through the pages of the Scriptures alone. He refuses to indulge in false perceptions concerning his worth, merit, or person; he is content to hide himself in the wounds of Christ and be found in Him alone.

144. 'No matter how much God is graciously pleased to increase our faith, indwelling unbelief will still be present to struggle against. It is just this element which renders the prayers of Scripture so pertinent to the saints of all ages: they exactly suit their case and express their sentiments.'

It is comforting to know that we don't have to have perfect faith to please our Father in heaven. He already knows that. Faith is a gift from God, and the Lord administers it to His saints in measure according to His pleasure. Therefore, while it is good and right to ask the Lord to increase our faith, it is wrong to be downcast because it is weak and occasionally

falters. Perhaps this is one way the Lord ensures that we will seek His presence and desire His fellowship when we realize we need Him every hour to strengthen and sustain us.

145. 'The fact is that many of the most spiritual prayers issue from those who regard themselves as being the least spiritual; yea, who seriously doubt if they have any spirituality at all. Unspiritual souls never pray for help against unbelief. It is much to be thankful for when we are made painfully conscious of our unbelief, for thousands of church-members never are so; and it is still greater cause for praise when we are honestly burdened thereby, and moved to pray for deliverance.'

It is God's design that He would be glorified in His saints. No other method will do nor suit the divine perfections of our Creator and Redeemer. We, on the other hand, are always apt to credit ourselves lavishly and heap accolades on our performances. This is not humility. Thus the Lord often allows us to fail morally so that we can see our dependence upon Him. When we seek His face in humility to restore us, He helps us and is subsequently glorified by us.

146. 'Ah, it is a grand thing when we are brought to the point where we realize that none but God Himself can subdue the workings of this evil in us. All self-help is

vain; all fellow creatures are powerless to render any relief—they cannot relieve themselves, still less others. Then "Cast thy burden upon the Lord, and He shall sustain thee" (Ps. 55:22).'

Sometimes as Christians, we erroneously think that 'casting our burdens on the Lord' is confined to trials and tribulations, outward difficulties and conflicts only. However, spiritual maladies are just as serious and burdensome to our souls, if not more than any external problem. Let us then cast every evil motive, every lustful thought or desire, every envious motion, every cowardly act, on the Lord. He will sustain us, not merely physically, but spiritually as well.

147. 'This is the strategic point where Satan concentrates his forces against us, and therefore it is here above all that we need Divine help. "Lord, I believe; help Thou mine unbelief": Lord, I do expect Thee to undertake for me, yet I am not able to exclude all doubting; I am persuaded of Thy power and pity, but enable me to rely upon Thee more fully and constantly.'

The great enemy of our souls knows us all too well. As the father of all pride, he knows which buttons in us to press to engender pride, worst of all spiritual pride, for that was the precise sin that spelled his doom. His pride elevated him to the inconceivable

notions of dethroning the Almighty Himself. O how dangerous is pride, Christian! Flee from it as Joseph fled from Potiphar's wife. It can ruin your reputation as well as your peace; but worst of all, it can ruin your usefulness for advancing the kingdom of God in your generation. For the weapons of our warfare are not carnal, but spiritual (2 Cor. 10:4). Remain clothed in humility and utterly dependent on the power of God.

148. 'We may apply our text ['Lord, I believe; help Thou mine unbelief'] to those seeking salvation. There may be a reader of this article who is halting between two opinions. He is convinced that Christ alone can meet his needs and satisfy his soul, yet he finds it so hard to give up the world and abandon his idols. He knows full well that in Christ alone is eternal life to be found, yet Satan still has such a hold upon him that he cannot surrender to the Lord Jesus and forsake the pleasures of sin. Then come to Him and say, "Lord, I believe; help Thou my unbelief". Or it may be, he feels himself to be such a godless wretch that he fears his case is hopeless: having sinned so grievously against light and privileges, he dares not venture upon the Gospel promises. Come to Christ and cry from the heart, "Lord, I believe; help Thou my unbelief."'

The gospel is a beacon of light and comfort to all who will have it. When did anyone in the Bible ever come

to Jesus only to leave unfulfilled and empty-handed? Never. When He looked out at the aimless multitude, the Bible says, He was moved with compassion because He viewed them as wandering sheep without a good shepherd (Matt. 9:36). When His own countrymen rejected Him, He wept and expressed how He wished to gather them under the safe haven of His wings, but tragically, they would have none of it (Matt. 23:37). There is no other friend like Jesus. O come to Him just as you are today.

JOHN MURRAY

149. 'The spiritual man is the person who is indwelt and controlled by the Holy Spirit, and a spiritual state of mind is a state of mind that is produced and maintained by the Holy Spirit.'

In contrast, the carnal man is the person who is dominated and controlled by the lust of the flesh. The carnal state of mind is opposition and hatred toward God and His ways (Rom. 8:7). There is no third category where I can be placed. To which of these do I belong, the spiritual or carnal state of mind? Search my heart, O God, and lead me on the right path.

150. 'He communes with his people and his people commune with him in conscious reciprocal love. "Whom having not seen you love," wrote the apostle Peter, "in whom, though now you see him not, yet believing, you rejoice with joy unspeakable and full of glory" (1 Pet. 1:8).'

How is it that I can love a Person that I have never seen? It seems a ridiculous and impossible thing. Yet it is true. If the Person of Christ did not exist, but was merely a character in a fable, He could not be loved as a living Person; but since He exists and we grasp Him by faith, we enjoy communion with the unseen Lord with exceeding joy that the world has never known. True, we have not seen Him, but we have tasted Him and experienced His goodness.